Talks on Texas Books

A Collection of Book Reviews

WALTER PRESCOTT WEBB. Photo courtesy of Russell Lee.

Talks on Texas Books

A Collection of Book Reviews

By WALTER PRESCOTT WEBB

Compiled and Edited
with an Introduction *by*
LLERENA FRIEND

Texas State Historical Association

Austin

Standard Book Number 87611–024–3

Library of Congress Catalog Card No. 76–84083

Copyright © 1970 Llerena Friend
  All rights reserved

Printed by Von Boeckmann-Jones
  Austin, Texas, U.S.A.

Table of Contents

Foreword

At a post-wedding party at the Headliners Club in Austin recently, one of the waiters drew me aside to talk about his self-imposed reading schedule.

"You know," he said, "I like that Dr. Webb best—he's so simple, so clear—he makes you understand, not like some of those writers who seem hell-bent on confusing."

Since I wanted to return to the festivities, I agreed. But before I could get away, the *maitre d',* a refugee from cotton-chopping who fought his way into his present eminence by intelligent use of the local library facilities, came alongside to tell how Dr. Webb had directed his reading when he had first joined the club. He also endorsed the simplicity of Webb's writings.

I would have liked to have stayed and argued whether Webb's writing *is* simple or possesses that high sophistication and care that passes for simplicity. To write with complexity is easy; to write with clarity is for most writers an everlasting chore, and for many an impossibility. Not even pages of simple declarative sentences will produce simple and easy understanding.

To avoid obscuring, Webb worked on his prose. In later years he told me that he had created a reasonably intelligent Bostonian who knew little of the regions or the cultures that Webb was writing about. And then he tried to explain his topics to that mythical person—he tried to make him see what Webb saw.

In other words, Webb wrote like a good teacher, with his students always uppermost in his mind. To him, the difference between being understood and just being read was the difference between art and writing. He wanted to be an artist, and he worked at it.

The little book which Llerena Friend has put together here shows the geneses of much of Webb's later ideas and activities. No one is better equipped than she to edit such a series of articles or to write a perceptive essay about the early Webb. She worked with him on his own projects, she wrote a fine dissertation that evolved into an enduring book under his loose supervision, and she talked techniques endlessly with him. She listened to most of his dreams, and she never hesitated to point out possible flaws in his logic or procedures.

On his part, Webb accepted Llerena Friend as a valued colleague and, of course, treated her always as a lady, in keeping with the Victorian margin of his upbringing. He let her "educate" him, as he always did with people he cherished, and in Miss Friend he turned loose a powerful personal educator. She can make facts attractive and suggestive, and she can be downright vehement in her pursuit of truth and motive.

However, what follows is not in the least a tribute from student-colleague to major professor. Llerena Friend's book is a tracing of the formation of young ideas by a mature man. (Webb, it should be noted, was probably never a young man, at least not until he passed 70, when he began to show signs of turning into a latent scampish Andy Hardy.)

These *Talks* make an intriguing book, and on behalf of the Texas State Historical Association I want to thank Llerena Friend for having brought it to us. We publish it, not as a sentimental gesture, but as a contribution to the realm of ideas in the Southwest.

JOE B. FRANTZ

Austin, Texas

Introduction

SINCE THE publication of *The Great Plains* in 1931, Walter Prescott Webb has not lacked recognition as writer and historian. Soon after that date, as demands came for public appearances and commencement addresses, he began to file the typescripts of most of the speeches and articles he prepared. In later years it was often simpler for him to have reprints made of magazine articles than to try to resurrect from the bottom of the pile on that cluttered desk the copy that some student or admirer or fellow historian requested. So post-1931 typescripts plus reprints constitute a considerable section of the Webb bibliography; less well-known writings and "literary remains" were buried in obscure or out-of-state periodicals. In some cases they deserve more than mere mention for the record.

Webb was forty-three years old when *The Great Plains* appeared, and he had been appearing in print since 1915— actually since that first letter in *The Sunny South* (1904) which won the attention of William E. Hinds and so proved to be, if not the most lucrative, perhaps the most rewarding writing of all.[1] He later analyzed that letter as having qualities of sim-

1. Walter Prescott Webb, "The Search for William E. Hinds," *Harper's Magazine* (July, 1961), 62–68. To be precise, his first printed piece, titled "Back Home" and signed W. Prescott Webb, appeared in the Breckenridge *Democrat* for August 13, 1903. Just before his graduation

plicity, directness, and honesty. Those same qualities appear in his talks to young people about Texas books, that were printed in the *Interscholastic Leaguer* between 1923 and 1928 and that are here reprinted. Eugene Manlove Rhodes, with whom Webb carried on a stimulating correspondence for the ten years before Rhodes' death in 1934, described Webb's writing as being "free from the stiff, the stilted, and the hi-faluting" and advised him to "have something to say, and say it in your own way." Recognizing that his Texas friend had a clear call to write, Rhodes advised: "Only one way to learn to punch cows and the same way to take the trail with wild ideas and dragging words, Yessir."[2]

From 1915 on Webb took the trail with various ideas, ideas not too wild to be corralled into three groupings: how to teach history (particularly the history of one's own area), the story of the Texas Rangers, and the meaning and significance of the Great Plains. For good measure some folklore was thrown in. Teaching was his profession; books and writing were his passion. Of books, he said on the day before his death: "They have been an obsession fully as absorbing to me as horse racing is to a compulsive horse player."[3] The editor of a magazine that had printed a piece of his fiction wrote him in 1924: "Also you might let us see the next story you turn out between History classes."[4] The greater part of his early writing was for history classes; perhaps he liked best what he turned out between those classes.

What follows here (in no sense a biography) is a summary

from the University of Texas, he sent to his home-town paper four articles about "The Story of Student Life in the University of Texas." These appeared in the Breckenridge *Democrat* for April 29, May 6, May 20, and May 27, 1915.

2. Rhodes to W. P. W., February 27, 1924, quoted in W. H. Hutchinson, *A Bar Cross Man* (Norman, Oklahoma, 1956), 207–208.

3. W. P. Webb, "The Confessions of a Texas Bookmaker," *Texas Libraries,* XXV, No. 3 (Fall, 1963), 88.

4. Charles Field to W. P. W., February 24, 1924. Webb Correspondence (University of Texas Archives, Austin, Texas).

of Webb's writings prior to the 1930's, excluding textbooks, book reviews, and certain articles on the Texas Rangers. What is included will show, I believe, the background for his contributions to Texas history, not only in books but in ideas. The evolutionary process was so natural and inevitable that it is impossible to say, "Here was born the Junior Historian movement," or "This is how the Texas Collection in the *Quarterly* evolved," or "From this unabashed and openly avowed love of a state came the dream of a *Handbook of Texas* to make brief, factual information about every aspect of that state available for every Texan from lawmaker to school child." Surely the Caldwell Prize in Local History and the Texas Book Talks with their pitch for the purchase of Texas books were the germination soil for the Junior Historians.

At the Conference on the Great Plains Area held in New York in 1942, Webb and J. Frank Dobie were participants. Webb spoke briefly about the Junior Historian movement, which he dated about 1939, and Dobie elaborated:

"I don't know but that when Webb gets to St. Peter he may not have more credit there for the Junior Historians of Texas than he will have for the books he has written, because the far-reachingness, if I may use such a word, of this Junior Historian move can't be determined at all. I merely go to the meetings. I have been to three. I have watched the growing enthusiasm of these young people with great pleasure, and I haven't seen anything in research of a sterner, more formal kind that seems to me at all so important as the spurring on through organization of these young people to a realization of their own cultural inheritance, which includes all sorts of history."[5]

Could there be a more poignant or poetic presentation of the pertinence of local history than the one in Webb's Foreword to H. B. Carroll's *Texas County Histories*?

5. Conference on the Great Plains Area, *Proceedings, April 17–18, 1942* (New York, 1942), 49–50.

"From my point of view, which always seems to me to be a most reasonable one, there is a great hidden university within a radius of five miles of every community. The geology is deeper than any well and the astronomy is firmament high. In between lie all the other branches of knowledge from the mysteries of religious experience to the mathematics of land surveys. The substance of science, art, and literature lie about and around us, things too big to be confined on the reservation. We shall have a real culture in Texas when we begin to see that this is so. . . .

"This bibliography is not going to effect any such revolution as I have hinted at. It is not suggested that there will be any quick transformation of the cultural pattern. Certainly no Texan, I least of all, would want Texas suddenly converted into Utopia, and thus isolated from the rest of the world. Perfection is entirely too uniform to suit a land which approaches perfection closest in its lack of uniformity. . . . I would not change Texas much if I could. She suits me just as she is, this eternal triangle of forest, desert, and plain. What I would do is to encourage study which would result in a better understanding and a deeper appreciation of Texas. . . .

"Now we must await the historian for whom the way has been prepared to write the Story of Texas, a story which ought to be true, not only in fact but in spirit and in flavor. This bibliography will never be far from his reach if he is to do what is expected. Such a book, when it comes, will complete the circuit and contribute in a thousand communities to a richer culture risen from the fertile soil of humble local histories."[6]

Perhaps there is another point to make. Webb's *Texas Rangers* first appeared in 1935. In 1957 Grossett & Dunlap, with far too little fanfare, published his *Story of the Texas Rangers,* not exactly a juvenile, but designed for older children and adults. Webb really preferred the junior book—as accurate as the ear-

6. H. Bailey Carroll, *Texas County Histories: A Bibliography* (Austin, 1943), xiii–xiv, xvii.

lier volume, presenting the best of the stories, "with the scholarship sandpapered off." The *Interscholastic Leaguer's* Book Talks were also for juveniles, and printed with a deliberate purpose, a purpose from which I believe more was achieved than the author ever realized. Two of the pieces reprinted here were not written by Webb. The L. W. Payne talk on *The Book of Texas* praises Webb as author of a capsule history of Texas. The other is Roy Bedichek's review of *The Great Plains,* a fitting climax to the series.

With the encouragement and financial assistance of that unseen friend named William E. Hinds, Walter P. Webb entered the University of Texas in the fall of 1909 and had two years of academic life before he returned to teaching a country school, this time at Brushy Knob in Throckmorton County for the term of 1911/1912. He was back in the University and used the facilities of the new Cass Gilbert Library building in 1912/1913. Not much of a joiner, he was attracted to the newly organized Texas Folk-Lore Society and served as its secretary in 1913/1914, when he was teaching at Beeville.[7] He was professionally minded and while at Beeville was a loyal and contributing member of the Texas State Teachers' Association. He had a three-months stint of varied duties at the Normal College at San Marcos before entering the University for his final year, taking his degree in June of 1915, when he was twenty-seven years old. In the fall of 1915 he was principal of the high school at Cuero, Texas, when, writing as W. Prescott Webb, he published in the *Journal of American Folklore* his "Notes on the Folk-Lore of Texas." He had gathered the material during his time at Beeville, and the article featured a Negro song (not all eighty stanzas), which he named, with conceit he said, "The African Iliad."[8]

7. J. Frank Dobie, "Folk-Lore in Texas and the Texas Folk-Lore Society," University of Texas *English Bulletin,* No. 10 (December, 1922), 27.

8. W. P. Webb, "Notes on the Folk-Lore of Texas," *Journal of American Folklore,* XXVIII (July–September, 1915), 290–299.

From Cuero also he submitted "Wild Horse Stories of South-west Texas" for the first volume of the *Publications of the Texas Folklore Society*. Again he drew on his experiences at Beeville. A charming snatch of his experience teaching the tenth grade at Cuero was presented in his Introduction to *Buck Schiwetz' Texas,* as he recalled how he ignored the Schiwetz absorption in drawing because he "made it a rule never to disturb a quiet student."[9] So Webb had had at least one article printed and another accepted when he attended the annual meeting of the Texas State Teachers' Association at Corpus Christi on November 26, 1915, and at the History Section of the Association presented a paper entitled "Increasing the Functional Value of History by the Problem Method of Presentation."[10] The paper ran to twenty-four pages in the *Texas History Teachers' Bulletin* and proved that teacher had done his home work. Another paper at that same meeting was read by Dr. Frederic Duncalf of the University of Texas History Department who was elected president of the section. Six teachers from San Antonio were present at the Corpus Christi meeting, and in the fall of 1916 Webb joined them for a two-year sojourn at Old Main Avenue High School in the Alamo City. During that time the United States entered the war to end wars, the one that ended up in history books as World War I.

In the spring of 1918 the editorial staff of the *Texas History Teachers' Bulletin* (alias the History Department of the University of Texas with Milton R. Gutsch as managing editor) decided to devote the November 1918 number to a discussion of the history of the war as it was being taught in Texas high schools. Questionnaires were sent to a number of secondary-

9. "Introducing Buck Schiwetz," in E. M. Schiwetz, *Buck Schiwetz' Texas* (Austin, 1960), 9.

10. W. P. Webb, "Increasing the Functional Value of History by Use of the Problem Method of Presentation," *Texas History Teachers' Bulletin,* IV, No. 2 [U.T. Bulletin 1916, No. 10], February 15, 1916, pp. 16–40. The bulletin, printed three times a school year, beginning in 1912, ran practical articles and suggestions on teaching, book lists, notes, and news of history teachers in Texas and elsewhere.

school teachers, including Webb, and his reply, "How the War Has Influenced History Teaching in San Antonio High Schools," was the lead article in the *Bulletin*. It concluded: "Not only are we in San Antonio teaching the past, but we are trying to point out the things we must do if we are to endure as a great nation. Perhaps it is not history, but it is what San Antonio and America need to know and do."[11]

As a San Antonio teacher, Webb had problems with the administration, and he began to cast about for a change of jobs. Professor Duncalf had held out hope that there would be a place at the University, but in April he had to write that the University administration, for the current year at least, would not "create a new place for history teaching." Duncalf urged his protégé to try for a year of graduate work, preferably not at Austin, and assured him: "Unless conditions change greatly, I am quite sure that we will have no difficulty next year, in getting such a position into the budget, which will make it much simpler."[12]

They did not have to wait that year. On October 8, 1918, Professor M. R. Gutsch proposed the establishment by the University of an agency to compile the Texas war records. His proposal was approved by the History Department on October 12, submitted to President R. E. Vinson in an informal conference on October 13, and approved by the Board of Regents on October 22.[13] The 1918/1919 *Staff Directory*, dated November 1, 1918, listed W. P. Webb as instructor in English history. This seemed to take care of the budget allocation. The 1918/1919 *Catalogue* carried Webb as instructor in history, and showed Charles W. Ramsdell teaching the "History of Eng-

11. W. P. Webb, "How the War Has Influenced History Teaching in San Antonio High Schools," ibid., VII, No. 1 [U.T. Bulletin 1864], November 15, 1918, p. 13.

12. F. Duncalf to W. P. W., April 23, 1918. Courtesy of Mrs. Walter Prescott Webb.

13. Texas War Records Collection, Miscellaneous File (University of Texas Archives, Austin).

land." A footnote indicated that Gutsch had been relieved of his teaching duties to direct the Texas War Collection. On November 11, 1918, Webb left his bookkeeping job in San Antonio and joined the history staff at the University in Austin.[14] By February, 1919, his name appeared in the list of *History Bulletin* editors. Volume VII, No. 3 of the *Bulletin* announced that Instructor Webb would teach two courses in the 1919 summer school: "The Early Middle Ages" and "The Feudal Age." In the 1919/1920 session he was assigned English history and History 9, a survey course in European history. His contribution to Bulletin VIII, No. 1, was called "A Lesson in Ancient History." His absorbing interest, however, was in a field far removed from that title, as he prepared his thesis on "The Texas Rangers in the Mexican War." He received the M.A. degree in June, 1920, and took on the title of adjunct professor of history. With the new degree and the new title he also took on two new courses: History 20, "The History of Civilization," which he taught in collaboration with Professor Duncalf, and Education 129, the "Teachers' Course in History." This "teaching teachers to teach" was what Duncalf had actually brought him to the University to do.

Webb has sometimes been classed as an interpretive historian. The first book review by him which I have found is related to that label. The book was Hutton Webster's *Modern European History*. After noting that early histories had stressed accounts of dynastic struggles, reviewer Webb wrote of the book by Webster:

". . . more recently there has been a tendency to 'interpret' history according to some formula. As a result of the latter we have geographical interpretations, economic, social, and what not. These historical alchemists of the last school have erred as widely as their precursors of the first, the chroniclers of intrigue

14. Tom B. Brewer, "A History of the Department of History at the University of Texas, 1883–1931" (M.A. thesis, University of Texas, 1957), 73.

and war. The true historian needs no touchstone. He considers all the factors, geographic, economic, social, and political, and gives to each the space and importance it seems to deserve. This is what Professor Webster has tried to do and with much success."[15]

With the May 1921 issue of the *Bulletin,* Webb became managing editor. He held the job for the remaining life of the publication, and under his management a shift came, without change of name, from a bulletin for teachers of history in Texas, to a bulletin for teachers of Texas history. A difference in tone and emphasis appeared immediately. Was it Webb or E. C. Barker who wrote an unsigned article on "Historical Research in Texas," which pointed out the opportunities for graduate study and historical research available in Austin, mentioned the García Library and the Littlefield Fund, and announced that the History Department at the University was offering the degree of Doctor of Philosophy? Whether or not he wrote that article, Webb did write a couple more book reviews. One was of Rolla Milton Tryon's *The Teaching of History in Junior and Senior High Schools,* which he was to use as a text in his course in "Teaching History." Labeling his other review "H. G. Wells as Historian," Webb selected extracts from *The Outline of History: Being a Plain Picture of the Life of Mankind* to give his readers an idea of Wells' presentation. His conclusion ran, "Of course the book will be criticised, but this much may be said for it—it will stimulate thought and reflection as no other modern book will."[16] That was nineteen years before Webb, in impresario role, secured Wells as a speaker for the Texas State Historical Association in Austin in November, 1940, and demonstrated his Midas touch for Association projects.[17]

Editor Webb allocated six pages of the November 1921 *Bul-*

15. *Texas History Teachers' Bulletin,* IX, No. 1 [U.T. Bulletin 2064], November 15, 1920, pp. 47–50.

16. Ibid., IX, Nos. 2 and 3 [U.T. Bulletin 2128], May 15, 1921, pp. 72–83.

17. W. P. Webb, *An Honest Preface* (Boston, 1959), 23–24.

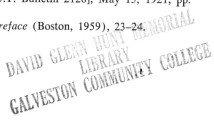

letin for Professor Tryon of the University of Chicago to discuss "Teaching Early European History." Then, because he was "always glad to render any service that will promote good teaching," he editorialized on the "Professional Book-Shelf," with recommendations for books on methods and some desirable maps and outlines as aids to teaching. Ere long he was to be preparing such outlines to accompany history texts. He also wrote two book reviews: of Eugene L. Hasluck's *The Teaching of History,* and Edward Raymond Turner's *Europe Since 1870.* Hasluck's book, from Cambridge University Press, was intended for teachers in England. Of the author's philosophy, Webb commented, "He does not want history held up as a panacea for human and social ills. He believes it will make us intelligent but not good; it will make us philosophers but not crusaders." Turner's book won commendation for ruthless elimination of the nonessential, for well-chosen source citations, and for maps.[18]

The editor made no contribution to the *Bulletin* for February, 1922, and no *Bulletin* was issued in May. A footnote to Volume XI, No. 1 reads: "No History Bulletin was issued for year 1922–23." That was the year that Webb did graduate work at the University of Chicago. In the fall of 1923 he was at home doing business at the old stand, a large room at the end of the old English Channel underneath the auditorium of the University of Texas Old Main Building. The *Texas History Teachers' Bulletin* became his vehicle for the promotion of investigation and writing of local history, a movement which was to culminate years later (he said he was always slow) in the Junior Historian movement and in *The Handbook of Texas.*

Bulletins XI, XII, XIII, and XIV were devoted almost exclusively to publicizing the Caldwell Prize in Local History and printing the prize-winning papers. In each issue the lead article which described the Caldwell Prize and the type of writing for which it would be awarded began with a quotation: "Evidently

18. *Texas History Teachers Bulletin,* X, No. 1 [U.T. Bulletin 2164], November 15, 1921, pp. 29–38.

the approach to history must begin nearer home and nearer now." The words were those of Logan Esarey, professor of Western history at Indiana University, whose article on "The Approach to History" was also printed when the writing contest was announced in April, 1923.[19] One of the University regents, C. M. Caldwell of Abilene, and the Dallas *News* cooperated to supply the prize money. The *News* believed the contest "an excellent idea and calculated to do good in that it will have the effect of familiarizing students with the history of the places in which they live." It was Managing-Editor Webb who listed the conditions and regulations of the contest, told how the essays would be judged, listed appropriate topics for local history, explored possible sources of information, and outlined the steps to be followed in the writing. That briefing was for high school students. To pin the matter down, an editorial was addressed "To the Teachers of History," for they alone could produce the desired results, even though their own returns might be intangible. As teacher was to pupil, the superintendent was to teacher, and the editor of the *Bulletin* would send to each county superintendent a sufficient number of *Bulletins* for distribution to each teacher interested in local history.

No information medium was to be omitted. Perchance the teacher might skip the Teachers' Association and not receive the *Bulletin;* the superintendent might have other matters on his mind. There was another avenue which led to almost every school in the state, *The Interscholastic Leaguer,* publicity vehicle for the University of Texas Interscholastic League. On December 15, 1923, the *Leaguer* carried a notice from Adjunct Professor of History W. P. Webb of a "Local History Prize Contest." While not to be conducted under the direction of the Interscholastic League, the League's director, Roy Bedichek, had endorsed the contest and offered space in the *Leaguer* for its promotion. In January, 1924, the *Leaguer* announced that Professor Webb had been "snowed under" by inquiries about

19. Logan Esarey, "The Approach to History," ibid., XI, No. 1 [U.T. Bulletin 2315], April 15, 1923, pp. 16–24.

the contest and elaborated on the subject by listing suitable subjects for local history. An editorial in March, 1924, stressed the contest as an unusual opportunity for cooperation between teachers of English and of history and described enthusiasm aroused in Anderson County and in Gainesville, Texas, where additional awards had been posted for the best examples of local history writing. The Webb editorial in the *Leaguer* for April 15, 1924, "Texas Frontier History," was essentially the first of his "Talks on Texas Books," albeit discussing a magazine, *The Frontier Times*.[20]

To get the contest off to a running start, the first *Leaguer* for the school year of 1924/1925, that for October, 1924, announced the winners and winning subjects in the Caldwell prize list for 1923/1924 and outlined plans for a similar but more extensive contest for the new year. Prize money was doubled by authorizing first and second prizes, to total $150, for the best essays submitted by teachers who were carrying on sound historical research in their own communities. The October 1924 *History Teachers' Bulletin* printed that first series of prize-winning essays, announced that at the History Section of the Texas State Teachers' Association at San Antonio in November Professor Webb would talk on "Opportunities for Research in Local History in Texas," and carried a two-page proposal for "A Library of Texas Books." For years Webb was to talk on specific books as additions to a dream "Texas Book Shelf" for every public school.[21] Transposed to the University of Texas, this was the primary articulation of the need for proper housing for the Texas Collection, such a spot as J. Frank Dobie was to call "A Corner Forever Texas."

The essays by the second group of prize winners in the Cald-

20. J. Marvin Hunter of *The Frontier Times* greatly appreciated the plug for his paper, a journal which he considered "different from anything of the kind yet published." J. M. H. to W. P. W., February 28, 1924, Webb Correspondence.

21. W. P. Webb, "The Texas Collection," *Southwestern Historical Quarterly*, XLII, No. 3 (January, 1939), 263–264.

well Contest were published in the *Texas History Teachers' Bulletin,* Volume XIII, in December, 1925. They filled 125 pages of the 139-page publication. The best historical writing by a teacher was announced as R. D. Holt's "A History of McCulloch County." There were personal notes on Texas history and Texas history teachers, and one page was devoted to "The Writing of County Histories." It was the editor's plea that the Texas Centennial (still a decade in the future) not be celebrated by thrashing over the old straw of history to provide the materials needed for the historical part of the Centennial celebration. Work should be under way, because the mastery of history required research and study. Each county had a history, in most cases unwritten. Teachers of history could use their local backgrounds to locate "the stuff from which histories may be written." Such a county history might also serve as the thesis for a Master's degree. In four short paragraphs he envisioned Centennial possibilities, teacher stimulation of pupil interest, the preservation of local history, and professional advancement.[22] When *The Handbook of Texas* was in preparation in the 1940's, the histories which resulted in part from that earlier exhortation furnished bibliography and points of departure for many *Handbook* entries. The prize essays for 1926 were published in *Bulletin* XIV, December, 1927, the last *History Teachers' Bulletin* to be issued. It was to be the topic of one of Webb's "Talks on Texas Books."

While setting teachers and students to competitive writing, the *Bulletin* editor was busy wielding his own pen, or rather was pecking speedily with two fingers at his own typewriter. Some of the writings went far afield; some remained for campus publication. With the postwar revival of the publication program of the Texas Folk-Lore Society, he was again a contributor. For Volume II (1923) he compiled a "Miscellany of Texas Folk-Lore." Volume III (1924) carried "The White Steed of the Prairies" and "The Legend of Sam Bass." In its preface,

22. *Texas History Teachers' Bulletin,* XIII, No. 1 [U.T. Bulletin 2546], December 8, 1925, p. 126.

Editor J. Frank Dobie, then teaching at Oklahoma A. & M., gave credit to Webb among those who had "verified certain references or run down certain information not procurable elsewhere than in the libraries of Texas material available at Austin." There were no Webb articles in *Happy Hunting Ground,* the publication for 1925, but Editor Dobie again mentioned Webb in his foreword: "The Texas Folk-Lore Society is by no means alone in its cultivation of the traditions and folk soil of the State. . . . At the University of Texas, Mr. W. P. Webb is promoting local history contests over the State, and the subject matter of the flood of papers he is receiving ranges from a battle to a ballad."[23]

It was Texas Folk-Lore Society Publication III, *Legends of Texas,* "a book the like of which has never been written in Texas," which Webb reviewed in his first article labeled "Talks on Texas Books" in the *Interscholastic Leaguer* for November, 1924. For the senior citizens he prepared another review of *Legends* for the *Southwestern Historical Quarterly* of January, 1925. Before the end of 1925 there were to be three other book talks: on *The Trail Drivers of Texas,* in December, 1924; on Andy Adams, *The Log of a Cowboy,* in January and February, 1925; and on John Lomax, *Cowboy Songs,* in March, 1925. A born teacher got in questions to stimulate interest, something about the author, a correlation between the book described and student's opportunity to locate things to talk about himself and enter in the history-writing contest. The Andy Adams classic merited two articles, the first ending with a good serial "come on" to generate interest for the next installment. To accompany the *Cowboy Songs,* more widely known than any other Texas book, a list of available sheet music and records was appended.

February, 1926, saw a departure in the form of the talks when the reviewer turned to direct discourse and the imagined conversation of boys on a hike as he sought to lure young readers to interest in a book on birds—and to interest in adding George

23. J. Frank Dobie (ed.), *Happy Hunting Ground* (Texas Folklore Society Publication IV), 1925, p. 8.

Finlay Simmons' *Birds of the Austin Region* to that hypotheti-
cal Texas Book Shelf. In complete contrast is the next "Book
Talk," a joint tribute to Stephen F. Austin and to the detective
historian, Eugene C. Barker, who wrote *The Life of Stephen
F. Austin.* Webb praises Barker's scholarship and good taste
and distinction in style in a moving style of his own:

"Stephen F. Austin—Father of Texas!

"For one hundred years—a whole century—Texas has been
too silent as to you! But at last that long silence is broken, and
in your own words, justice has been done you. Perhaps this
silence has been too long, or perhaps it has taken Texas one
hundred years to produce him who could do you full justice,
who could set you forth in keeping with your work and sacrifice."

The review is revealing, not only of Austin and Barker but
of the relationship of Barker and Webb. When the University
honored Dr. Webb at the time of the publication of *The Great
Frontier,* Dr. Barker was one of the speakers. He characterized
his colleague as an original and thoughtful historian, a wise and
efficient teacher. He said that he had always been proud of
Webb's books and "grateful for the intelligence that taught me
early in my acquaintance with Webb not to interfere with his
freedom to do his own work in his own way." His gratitude was
for more than thirty years of comradeship of a stimulating,
helpful, and understanding friend.[24] As was the wont of members of the History Department, Webb referred to Dr. Barker
as "Chief." In his gift copy of *The Great Plains,* sent to Barker
at Boulder, Colorado, his sentiment was—"To the Chief, who
had he been a Plains Indian, would have ridden at the head of
his tribe." Webb was chairman of the committee which prepared the Barker "In Memoriam" for the University Faculty
Minutes, and its content reveals his authorship.

The September 1926 "Book Talk" was a brief but sincere

24. Dallas *News,* November 30, 1952.

appreciation of the reference value of Z. T. Fulmore's *History and Geography of Texas as Told in County Names*, a worthy candidate for a less-than-five-foot shelf to hold good Texas books. The next month's *Leaguer* talk was devoted to Volume V of the Texas Folk-Lore Publications. Webb summed up his sampling of the contents by saying, "There is something in this volume of folklore that will interest everyone, the material in it comes from the Texas soil, and it has all the variety and raciness of that soil." In January, 1927, the bookish conversation concerned Frank S. Hastings' *A Ranchman's Recollections,* with a dividend in the form of an exchange between Webb and the *Leaguer's* editor, Roy Bedichek. After Bedichek's death, Webb wrote "Dear Bedi" for *The Texas Observer,* recalling that Editor Bedichek of the San Antonio *Express* had once refused him a job as a reporter and also that he had spent a five-year stretch on the Interscholastic League Council.[25] That was 1930 to 1935.

The editor did not get another talk from his "free horse" for over a year, when the February 1928 *Leaguer* summarized the winners in the most recent Caldwell local history contest. In November, 1928, Webb used his space to editorialize on his favorite topic, a Texas Book Shelf, and then confessed that he was continuing his column because "a new book has just appeared that is so different from anything that came before it that I cannot resist the temptation to tell you about it." The book was *Texas Wild Flowers* by Ellen D. Schulz, one of Webb's fellow teachers at Main Avenue High School in San Antonio in 1916.[26] What fun he must have had with his conclusion when he faulted the book for not having been written when he was "a small boy roaming the fields and prairies of West Texas."

The last of Webb's "Talks on Texas Books" appeared in December, 1928, and concerned L. W. Payne's *Survey of Texas*

25. Ronnie Dugger (ed.), *Three Men in Texas* (Austin, 1967), 84.
26. W. P. Webb, "San Antonio Teachers," *Texas Libraries,* XXV, No. 3 (Fall, 1963), 97.

Literature, the publication of which he considered a good sign that the history of the state was sufficiently long to justify a book about Texas books. Payne's preface had mentioned Webb as one of the friends who had read the manuscript and helped make suggestions and corrections. In his discussion of books on Texas Rangers, Payne had written: "Professor Walter P. Webb of the University of Texas has in preparation an exhaustive history of the Rangers, and no doubt his authoritative contribution will soon be added to the long list of books dealing with that daring, intrepid, romantic, and effective body of mounted men known all over the western world as the Texas Rangers."[27]

But the Rangers had to wait while Webb told the story of the Great Plains, which captured priority in his thinking although it was certain aspects of the Rangers' weapons and responsibilities which diverted his attention to the region. In the spring of 1928 he took a semester's leave from teaching to devote full time to the book on the Plains, but, in what was to become his *modus operandi,* he sent out some trial balloons in the form of monographs on his topic. "Land and Life of the Great Plains" appeared in Volume IV (1928) of *The West Texas Historical Association Year Book.* The next year, "The Great Plains and the Industrial Revolution" was in the *Trans-Mississippi West,* published in Boulder, Colorado. The second number of the *Panhandle Plains Historical Review* (1929) featured "The Great Plains Block the Expansion of the South." In these last three publications, three sections of the area involved learned aspects of their history.

Meanwhile, back on the campus, Professors Barker, Payne, L. L. Click, and others, made their contributions to the *Leaguer's* "Talks on Texas Books," for it was a mark of the University faculty of the period to assist and encourage colleagues and to participate in all of the University side activities, such as the projects of the Interscholastic League. Payne's contribution in October, 1929, concerned *The Book of Texas,* to

27. L. W. Payne, *A Survey of Texas Literature* (Chicago, 1928), vii, 10.

which Webb contributed the first article, described by Payne as "an interesting and well-written condensation of the whole of the romantic history of Texas under her six flags." The author of that article was busy promoting graduate work in the History Department, in which he was teaching new courses. History 55 was a survey of the later period of American history, and in 1929/1930 he offered for the first time a course called "The Great Plains and the Rocky Mountains." From his own work on the subject and from the activities of his students, whom he described as digging holes all over the Great Plains, came the book discussed by Bedichek in January, 1932, when "Talks on Texas Books" featured *The Great Plains* by Walter Prescott Webb. He had conceived the series of "Talks on Texas Books." His own book completed the series.

LLERENA FRIEND

Texas Frontier History

The *Frontier Times*

THE EDITOR of the *Leaguer*[1] recently suggested that I talk with his readers about interesting historical subjects. I shall do this in a very informal manner, and with the purpose of introducing them to the best books and magazines dealing with the history and the tradition of Texas. There is no reason why every boy and girl should not find an interest in Texas history. The reason they do not is because they do not have access to many of the best things that have been done. A textbook alone is not sufficient for historical instruction. A history text deals with the important things rather than with those of absorbing interest. Furthermore, the things that are treated are important, usually, to grown people, and not to school students. Textbook writers would be glad to put in more interesting incidents, but they do not have the space. They hope that the students will supplement the text with other readings and thereby widen their view of history and their knowledge of the subject. I propose to discuss some of these interesting supplementary readings.

Interscholastic Leaguer, April, 1924.

1. The editor of the *Leaguer* in 1924 was Roy Bedichek, whose history of the League is called *Educational Competition: The Story of the University Interscholastic League of Texas* (Austin, 1956). For the Webb-Bedichek relationship see Ronnie Dugger (ed)., *Three Men in Texas* (Austin, 1967).

*Frontier Times*² is a monthly magazine published by J. Marvin Hunter of Bandera, Texas, which would be read with pleasure by every red-blooded Texas boy. The editor says that his purpose is to publish "a magazine devoted to frontier history, border tragedy, and pioneer achievement," and every issue so far shows that the editor is achieving his purpose. The magazine is devoted almost exclusively to Texas history, early frontier history, and most of the articles in it are written by "old-timers" who have had thrilling experiences in Texas. The titles of the articles for February are typical:

> An Early Day Sheriff's Experience.
> Indian Attack near Uvalde.
> The Heroism of a Faithful Negro Slave.
> The Battle of Antelope Hills.
> Found a Wounded Indian.
> "Slick" Clements Was a Good Marksman.
> John Fleutsch, a Frontier Justice.
> The Killing of Sam Bass.
> "Wild Bill" Hickok.

Each of these articles is rich in incident and local color of Texas history, as the following article will illustrate. The author of this article, now dead, was a printer, newspaperman, Texas Ranger, and Confederate soldier. With all the experience he had the ability to tell a true story in an interesting fashion. It is by Taylor Thompson and entitled: "Found a Wounded Indian."

"In the autumn of 1864 with a party of six men I was crossing what is known as the 'Big Divide' between the present site of Junction City, before there was ever a house built there, however, and the headwaters of Johnson's fork of Guadalupe.

2. The *Frontier Times* began publication in October, 1923. The Taylor Thompson story related here appeared in Vol. I, No. 5 (February, 1924), p. 16. For thirty years Webb was a subscriber and sometime contributor to the original *Frontier Times*. With its revival under Joe Small, he was one of the first ten subscribers to the 1958 publication, and he served as historical consultant until his death.

It is about twenty-five miles across the big divide and no stream or water course runs through it. We had filled out canteens and water gourds, however, and when about four miles from the Guadalupe river we stopped to eat a midday meal. There was a small grove of liveoak trees surrounded by a thick grove of liveoak runners, which made a dense thicket covering about one acre, near where we stopped. Soon after we halted, I noticed a number of buzzards perched on the trees in a thicket where others were flying about in the vicinity. I called the attention of my comrades to those foul birds, and suggested that there was probably some animal dead or dying in the thicket. After we had eaten dinner, my curiosity having been aroused, I picked up my rifle and started to the thicket, determined to investigate. Macedonio (probably a Mexican guide) called as I started, 'Look out, sergeant, there may be a wounded Indian in that thicket.' I paid no attention to the old man, however, though, of course I kept a sharp lookout, and I had not penetrated far into the thicket before I came upon a wounded Indian. One of his legs had been broken by a gunshot and he had received two other wounds, one in the shoulder and one in the side of his face. His bow and quiver of arrows as well as the tomahawk or hatchet were lying by his side, and he had a long butcher knife in his belt. When I approached him he tried to get his bow in position to shoot, but he was so weak he could not do so. I spoke to him in Spanish but he made no reply, merely staring at me without batting an eye. I returned and told my companions of my discovery and we all repaired to the scene. I suppose the wounded Indian thought we were going to kill him, but after working with him for some time we induced him to drink from a water gourd one of the men held to his lips. Then one of the men gave him some dried beef which he ate greedily. We then rigged up a horse litter, placed the Indian on it and carried him to the nearest water, about four miles away. There we made a bed for him by the side of a small rivulet upon which we laid him. We left a tin cup with him with which he could reach the water and also left three or four pounds of

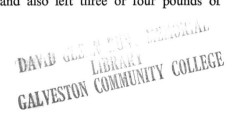

dried meat with him. Some of my men wanted to kill him but I talked them out of that idea. And I finally induced old Macedonio to dress his wounds and bandage them up in a rude fashion. There was not a ranch nearer than thirty miles or I would have carried him there and there was probably not a doctor nearer than San Antonio, more than 100 miles away. We rode away and left him in the wilderness. We passed there again three days later and the wounded Indian was gone, though we searched the vicinity closely we found no trace of him. What became of him we never knew, but I have always believed that some of his companions were watching us when we carried him away and that they followed on our trail, found the wounded companion and carried him off."

This little story is told in language that will not meet the full approval of the grammarian, but it has in it a reality, a romance that is more appealing than correct sentences. Besides there is much information about the Texas frontier in it. The following questions may be answered:

> Where is the Guadalupe River?
> Where is Junction?
> How was the Indian armed?
> How did early Texans carry water?
> What is a horse litter?
> What did the Texans have to eat?
> How thickly was Texas populated around Junction in 1864?
> Why did some of the Texans want to kill the wounded Indian?

And for those who must have a moral adorn a good tale: Did the Texans do right in treating the Indian kindly? If I am not mistaken, J. Marvin Hunter's *Frontier Times* contains real Texas history, the sort boys like.

Talks on Texas Books

I ·

Legends of Texas

THE PURPOSE OF this column in the *Leaguer* is to stimulate the interest of Texas boys and girls in local history, that is
the history of their town, county, or community, or of some
person in that community. A full discussion of the [Caldwell
local history] contest is set forth in the *History Teachers' Bulletin,* together with directions as to how to gather and write local
history. There will be ten cash prizes, ranging from $40.00 to
$7.50, given to the high school students who submit the best
essays or articles on local historical subjects. From month to
month this column will contain announcements and notices pertaining to the contest, and those interested should follow these
announcements.

The principal feature of this department, however, will not
be the discussion of the contest, but of those things which per-
tain to and aid local historical investigation. This year the
Leaguer program will consist of a discussion of Texas books
and Texas authors. I shall go upon the assumption that every
student would be glad to know more about his native State.
This information can be had best from those men and women
who have written of the State. Each month then, I propose to
take up a Texas book or a Texas author and talk to you in-
timately about this book and author. Some of the books will be

Interscholastic Leaguer, November, 1924.

historical; some will be fiction; most of them were written by Texans; all by men who have an intimate knowledge of what they write; and most important, each book discussed can now be purchased from the publisher or from book stores. There are many other excellent books about Texas, but most of them are out of print and can only be obtained secondhand, and often at great expense. Furthermore, these books are chosen in the belief that they will aid many students in their local historical investigation, that they will give the student a better appreciation of his native State and a better understanding of important phases of Texas history.

It would indeed be a fine thing if every public school in Texas would place in its library a number of the worthwhile books on Texas. Students may learn something of the books and their authors through this column, but they can learn very little at best. They should have an opportunity to handle the books, to read them, and to study them at will. The books can be placed in the library at a small initial cost where they would remain permanently to serve and delight coming generations of students. There is no investment that would be more worthy. Those interested should talk the matter over with their English teachers and history teachers, and with the librarian and principal. They will be glad to suggest ways and means by which a library of Texas books may be built. The first book on the program is *Legends of Texas.*

HERE IS A BOOK the like of which has never been written in Texas. It is a book that will have a permanent value and an important place in the future in any discussion of Texas literature or tradition. The book cannot be said to have an author, because it is folklore, which comes from among the folk, the people. Everybody has heard folklore: stories of buried treasure, tales of haunted houses, or fantastic accounts of how rivers, towns, or flowers received their names. All of us know of some interesting person in the community who is a regular storehouse of ghost stories, traditions, and legends. From these persons Professor J. Frank Dobie, together with about forty assistants scattered over the State, gathered all these fantastic accounts that could be obtained, sifted them, selected the most interesting ones, and incorporated them in a handsome blue volume which bears the suggestive title, *Legends of Texas*. It is a book that will appeal to teachers, parents, and students, and this wide appeal is due to the fact that each person will find in it something that he heard as a child, something that is fundamental to the race and to Texas. There have been many legends gathered. Washington Irving deftly turned the legends of the Hudson River region into literature that will not perish. Longfellow sought in Indian legend the inspiration and the materials for his songs of Hiawatha; and even the great Shakespeare made use of legend, of witches and ghosts and spirits—veritable folklore—in his plays. As yet no one has used the legends of Texas in a high literary fashion. In fact, up until this time they have not been available. But now they are gathered together between the covers of a book, and there is little doubt that they will serve as the basis of many literary efforts. Thus, in time they will become of immense importance to the students of Texas literature.

In order to give some idea of the variety and nature of these legends I will tell briefly of a few of them. There is a large number of them devoted entirely to buried treasure. How many of us have heard that Spaniards and Mexicans buried gold in Texas? How many have not seen the places where treasure hunters came to dig in the night in the hope of finding buried gold? Perhaps in the northern and western part of the State, we hear of the loot buried by Sam Bass, or the James boys; if on the coast, we hear tales of the pirate Lafitte. All of these stories find a place in *Legends of Texas*.

A second group, more interesting than the first, deals with the supernatural. Here are all the creepy ghost and ghostly tales of Texas. One tells us of a place in Crosby County known as Stampede Mesa, where cattlemen claim that on dark nights they can see a herd of phantom steers stampeding over the

mesa led by a "murdered ghost, astride a blind-folded horse."
Then there is the story of the "Death Bell of the Brazos," and
of the "Padre's Beacon," a ghostly light that marked the en-
trance of Trinity River. There are of course legends of lovers.
Lovers' leaps and lovers' retreats abound all over the State, and
most of them have romantic stories connected with their past.
Here we find the story of the Enchanted Rock in Llano County,
Lovers' Retreat in Palo Pinto, Lover's Leap in Kimble County
(with illustrations), and several others. These are followed by
stories of Lafitte the Pirate, the legend of the bluebonnet and
of other flowers, and finally a number of miscellaneous legends
that do not seem to fit into the other sections.

Professor J. Frank Dobie, editor of the *Legends of Texas,*
spent more than three years ransacking the State for the materials incorporated in his book. Professor Dobie is a native Texan,
educated at Southwestern University at Georgetown and at Columbia University. Formerly he taught English at the University
of Texas, but he is now at the A. & M. College, Stillwater,
Oklahoma. He expects to continue gathering Texas legends and
will be glad to hear from any Texas boy or girl who knows one
that is interesting.

Legends of Texas was published by the University of Texas
Press and is now going into the second edition. The book sells
for $2.50,[3] and may be obtained from Miss Ethel Burch, Secre-
tary of the Texas Folk-Lore Society, University Station, Austin,
Texas.

3. Those who purchased the books reviewed in these "Talks" were to
realize financial as well as cultural dividends. As the books went out of
print and collectors became "Texana" conscious, the original editions
commanded prices far removed from the original quotations.

II ·

The Trail Drivers of Texas

THIS BOOK is [compiled] by George W. Saunders. Who were the Trail Drivers of Texas? How many can guess? Many of the readers of the *Leaguer* live on the old trails, obliterated now, which were made in the days after the Civil War by the Texas Trail Drivers.

The Trail Drivers were those men who engaged in the business of driving large herds of cattle from Texas to the northern markets, to Kansas and points farther north, in the days when there were not enough railroads to haul the cattle. The trail leading from Texas northward bore several names, Texas Trail, Texas Trace, Cattle Trail, but the name by which it is most familiarly known in the Chisholm Trail. It received this name because a man named Chisum was one of the first men to drive over a part of the trail, and in later years his name was applied to the whole cattle trail.

In the spring of the year the cattle were rounded up on the Texas range and started slowly north, accompanied by a number of cowboys, a foreman, horse wrangler, and a chuckwagon managed by the cook. It took from three to five months to make the trip, depending upon the place the herd started from in Texas and its destination in the north. Some herds were driven as far as Canada. The herds moved very slowly, and made their

Interscholastic Leaguer, December, 1924.

living on the range as they went. There were no fences and the cattle could scatter over a wide area and graze, but all the time the herders kept them drifting in a northerly direction.

The beginning of the cattle drives from Texas was in 1867, immediately after the close of the war between the North and the South. During the war vast herds had accumulated in Texas, where the climate was warm enough for them to winter on the range. In Texas, cattle were worth nothing, but beef was scarce in the North, and it was not long before Texas ranchers found that they had an unlimited market for what had seemed to be worthless. From the Texan's point of view the cow was important because cattle could transport themselves to the distant market. Nothing else in Texas had much commercial value. The cattle were driven along the edge of the prairie, west of all settlements. The ranchman soon realized the westward-moving settlers would shortly occupy the range and with farms and fields close the trail to the cattle herds. The process of closing the trail was hastened in the early eighties, by the increasing use of barbed wire, which had not long been invented. The settlers and the barbed-wire fences pushed the herds farther and farther west until finally, in 1895, it was impossible for a herd to go up the trail any more. Another cause had begun to operate also, and that was the construction of railroads into the West. By 1895 railroad transportation had been provided for all parts of the country and the day of trail driving was over.

The cattle trail, then, originated about 1867; it ceased to exist in 1895. During that time hundreds of herds and millions of cattle went from Texas to northern markets on their own hoofs. There has never been in all the world anything to compare with this migration of man with his cattle. Around the herd was romance, adventure, hard work, and plenty of excitement for everyone.

The complete story of the men who drove cattle out of Texas is told by the men themselves, now old men, in *The Trail Drivers of Texas,* a book compiled by George W. Saunders, president of the Trail Drivers' Association. The book is printed in two volumes, and is made up of some three hundred articles by as many of the men who actually drove cattle out of Texas. This book constitutes what the historian calls a primary source. It is absolutely the best source there is on the cattle trail. It deals with all subjects pertaining to the cattle drives: stampedes, Indian fights, camp life. The first volume is by far the better one. The books sell for $3.00 per volume or $5.00 for the set, and may be had by addressing Mr. George W. Saunders, San Antonio, Texas. It should be said that the proceeds from the sale of the books go into a fund for the erection of a monument to those Texans who drove cattle from the State to northern markets.

Add to that Texas book collection on the Texas Shelf in the high school library *The Trail Drivers of Texas.*

N.B.: Inquire of your parents and neighbors for some person in your community who was a Trail Driver. These old Trail Drivers can tell you some interesting stories which you may use effectively in the local history contest, discussed briefly in another space. Ask your history teacher to tell you about the prizes which are offered for essays about interesting persons and places in your community. The prizes range from $7.50 to $40.00, and the essays will be published in the Dallas *News.* For particulars address W. P. Webb, University of Texas.

III and IV ·

The Log of a Cowboy

Part One

THE PURPOSE of this series of articles is to present to the readers of the *Leaguer* brief descriptions of certain Texas books in the hope that the high schools will set aside in their libraries a shelf to be known as the "Texas Book Shelf." Upon this shelf should be placed the most interesting and important books about Texas. The two books discussed heretofore are

1. *Legends of Texas,* edited by J. Frank Dobie.
2. *Trail Drivers of Texas,* edited by George W. Saunders.

The book discussed this month will perhaps make more interesting reading than either of the other two. It is *The Log of a Cowboy,* by Andy Adams.

ANDY ADAMS was himself one of the trail drivers of Texas. He came to Texas in the early eighties, when the exodus of cattle from Texas was at its height. For several years Mr. Adams, or Andy Adams as he is called by his admirers, went up the trail each season as cowboy or foreman of a Texas herd. Later, Andy went into the mining business in Colorado, and when he was about forty years old the idea occurred to him to

Interscholastic Leaguer, January, 1925.

set down his experiences in Texas and on the trail. Without doubt there were many men who drove cattle that knew as much as Andy Adams about the cattle industry and about Texas. But not one of them had the imagination, the memory, the literary skill to transfer their experiences from their minds to the pages of books. In the course of time, he wrote a number of books, most of which concerned Texas. Some of these are *The Texas Matchmaker, The Outlet, Cattle Brands,* and *Reed Anthony, Cowman.* But the best book written by Andy Adams is *The Log of a Cowboy.*

The Log of a Cowboy is a novel, yet it was written with such fidelity to truth, with such naturalness, that it has passed with many for a history of a cattle drive. We have heard of the painter whose portrait of a curtain fooled an artist, and of the one whose portrait of grapes fooled the birds, and we have considered that such portraits must have been excellent. Andy Adams has written of cattle so well that he has fooled historians, novelists, and even cowboys. What Andy Adams wrote for fiction, these people have taken for fact, and one of the most prominent novelists of our day, a man who should have known better, referred to Andy Adams' books as quasi-fiction, or half fiction. That was unfair to Andy Adams, because a novelist wants his books to be recognized as novels, as literature rather than history.

It is only in recent years that the cattle-driving days of Texas have attracted much attention. The United States government has employed a man to write an authentic history of the Texas cattle trade, and that man has spent considerable time at the University of Texas examining the records of the trade that are to be found in the Texas Library. Emerson Hough's book, *North of 36,* together with the moving picture drama based upon the book, has attracted much attention. Both book and picture do very well, but it is safe to say that Andy Adams has written a far better book than Emerson Hough wrote, a book that is destined to be recognized as the classic of the Texas cattle drive. I propose to give a brief review of the book and some extracts from it, which should make you want to read the whole book and place it on your Texas Book Shelf, where other boys and girls may find it and enjoy it as you will.

The book opens with a group of cowboys gathered on the banks of the Rio Grande to receive a herd of cattle from Mexico. These cattle, together with others from Texas, are to be driven from Brownsville to the Blackfoot Indian Agency in Montana. The herd goes under the Circle Dot brand, which is a circle with a dot in the middle, and it is owned by two men, Lovell and Flood. Flood's orders to his men before they left Brownsville were as follows:

"Boys, the secret of trailing cattle is never to let your herd know that they are under restraint. Let everything that is done be done voluntarily by the cattle. From the moment you let them off the bed ground in the morning until they are bedded at night, never let a cow take a step, except in the direction of its destination. In this manner, you can loaf away the day, and cover from fifteen to twenty miles, and the herd in the meantime will enjoy all the freedom of the open range."

Then follows what almost amounts to a day-by-day record of the progress of the Circle Dots from Brownsville up by San Antonio, Austin, Fort Worth, and other Texas points, and on to Montana. There was much suffering on the trail, and one of the remarkable chapters is "The Dry Drive," which was made in the western country about a week's drive above San Antonio. I cannot give a full account of this drive, but will take up in the next issue of the *Leaguer* the narrative after it was well under way, after the cattle had begun to suffer for water.

PART TWO

As PROMISED in the last issue of the *Leaguer,* I shall continue the description given by Andy Adams in his *Log of a Cowboy,* of the dry drive.

Interscholastic Leaguer, February, 1925.

"Several times for an hour or more, the herd was allowed to lie down and rest, but by the middle of the afternoon thirst made them impatient and restless, and the point men (men who rode in the lead) were compelled to ride steadily in the lead in order to hold the cattle to a walk. A number of times during the afternoon we attempted to graze them, but not until twilight of evening was it possible . . .

"We were handling the cattle as humanely as possible under the circumstances. The guards for the night were doubled, six men on the first half and the same on the latter, Bob Blades being detailed to assist Honeyman in night-herding the saddle horses. If any of us got more than an hour's sleep that night he was lucky. Flood, McCann, and the horse wranglers did not even try to rest. To those of us who could find time to eat, our cook kept open house. Our foreman knew that a well-fed man can stand an incredible amount of hardship, and appreciated the fact that on the trail a good cook is a valuable asset. Our outfit was therefore cheerful to a man, and jokes and songs helped to while away the weary hours of the night. . . .

"In spite of our economy of water, after breakfast on this third morning there was scarcely enough left to fill the canteens for the day. In view of this, we could promise ourselves no mid-day meal—except a can of tomatoes to the man—so the wagon was ordered to drive through to the expected water ahead. . . . The day turned out to be one of torrid heat, and before the middle of the forenoon the cattle lolled their tongues in despair, while their sullen lowing surged through from rear to lead and back again in piteous yet ominous appeal. The only relief we could offer was to travel them slowly, as they spurned every opportunity offered them to lie down. . . .

"Good cloudy weather would have saved us, but in its stead was a sultry morning without a breath of air, which bespoke another day of sizzling heat. We had not been on the trail more than two hours before the heat became almost unbearable to man and beast. Had it not been for the condition of the herd, all might yet have gone well, but over three days had now elapsed without water for the cattle, and they became feverish and ungovernable. The lead cattle turned back several times, wandering aimlessly in any direction, and it was with considerable difficulty that the herd could be held on the trail. The rear overtook the lead, and the cattle gradually lost all semblance of a trail herd. Our horses were fresh, however, and after about two hours' work we once more got the herd strung out in trailing fashion, but before a mile had been covered the leaders again turned, and the cattle congregated into a mass of unmanageable animals, milling and lowing in their fever and thirst. The milling only intensified their sufferings from the heat, and the outfit split and quartered them again and again, in the hope that this unfortunate outbreak might be checked. No sooner was the milling stopped than they would surge hither and yon, sometimes half a mile, as ungovernable as the waves of an ocean. After wasting several hours in this manner, they finally turned back over the trail, and the utmost efforts of every man in the outfit failed to check them. We threw our ropes in their faces, and when this failed, we resorted to shooting; but, in defiance of the fusillade and the smoke, they walked sullenly through the line of horsemen, across their front. Six-shooters were discharged so close to the leaders' faces as to singe their hair, yet, under a noonday sun, they disregarded this and every other device to turn them, and passed wholly out of our control. In a number of instances wild steers deliberately walked against our horses, and then, for the first time, a fact dawned on us that chilled the marrow in our bones—*the herd was going blind.*"

It is a remarkable passage, this description of a dry drive, in which a herd of 3,000 cattle go blind and pass entirely from under the control of the men in charge. The result was that the cattle went on the back trail until they found water and, after a short rest, regained their sight and were then taken by another route.

But all of the book is not so vivid. At night, when all was

going well, the men gathered around the campfires and told stories. Andy Adams has woven in here the stories that were actually told. There is death, and gambling, and shooting on the trail, but the author gives these incidents and events with a simplicity and naturalness that puts to shame the writers of sensational cowboy stuff served up in many books and magazines. *The Log of a Cowboy* is the very spirit of the cattle trail, captured better by Andy Adams than by any other writer.

Andy Adams lives today at the Alamo Hotel at Colorado Springs, Colorado. He is no longer a young man, but he retains the spirit of youth, and it would delight him to have the readers of the *Leaguer* write him. He has been away from Texas now for a long time, but he loves the State where he spent his youth and which inspired him to do his best work. His books are published by Houghton-Mifflin Company, Boston, and sell for $2 each.

P.S. Andy Adams describes in his books many of the places mentioned by the students last year in their essays on local history. For example, he describes the passage of the herd at Doan's Crossing on Red River. Anita F. Dickinson, of Vernon, wrote an essay on Doan's that won a special mention prize in the contest. This essay is now published with nineteen others in *The History Teachers' Bulletin,* and will be sent to any high school student upon request. This bulletin also contains rules and regulations for the contest for this year.

V ·

Cowboy Songs

UP TO THE PRESENT I have attempted to give the boys and girls who read the *Leaguer* an impression of the following Texas books:

> Dobie, *Legends of Texas*.
> Saunders, *Trail Drivers of Texas*.
> Andy Adams, *The Log of a Cowboy*.

I now desire to present what is probably the most widely known Texas book: *Cowboy Songs* by John A. Lomax.

It is not too much to say that Mr. Lomax' *Cowboy Songs* is more widely known than any other Texas book, especially in the North and East. Mr. Lomax, who lives in Austin, is often called to northern colleges and universities to read and sing the cowboy songs. He has had extensive experience on the ranches, has lived in the cowcamps, and gathered the songs everywhere that they could be found.

Every Texas boy and girl will enjoy reading these cowboy songs. Many of you know the tunes to these songs from having heard them sung by the boys in the country. You may be interested to know that it is almost impossible for outsiders to learn to sing these songs. One must learn them on the range or from range people, or not at all. I do not propose to give

Interscholastic Leaguer, March, 1925.

you a lengthy discussion of the book that contains them. It is much better to give you samples of the songs themselves. Before doing that, however, I wish to tell you what Theodore Roosevelt said about them in a letter which he wrote to Mr. Lomax. Among other things he wrote:

"You have done a work emphatically worth doing and one which should appeal to the people of our country, but particularly to the people of the West and Southwest. Your subject is not only exceedingly interesting to the student of literature, but also to the student of the general history of the West."

The first ballad in the book is one that is widely known; one that once heard cannot be forgotten.

THE DYING COWBOY

"O bury me not on the lone prairie,"
These words came low and mournfully
From the pallid lips of a youth who lay
On his dying couch at the close of day.

He had wailed in vain, till o'er his brow
Death's shadows fast were gathering now;
He thought of his home and his loved one nigh
As the cowboys gathered to see him die.

"O bury me not on the lone prairie,
Where the wild coyotes will howl o'er me,
In a narrow grave just six by three—
O bury me not on the lone prairie.

"O bury me not—" and his voice failed there,
But we took no heed of his dying prayer;
In a narrow grave just six by three
We buried him there on the lone prairie.

The following ballad, entitled "The Cowboy's Life," has much of the spirit and thought of the cowboy. It bears, however, evidences of authorship. By that I mean that it is the work of one person, probably in this case, of James Barton Adams.

The Cowboy's Life

The bawl of a steer
To a cowboy's ear
   Is music of sweetest refrain;
And the yelping notes
Of the gray coyotes
   To him are a glad refrain.

And his jolly songs
Speed him along,
   As he thinks of the little gal
With golden hair,
Who is waiting there
   At the bars of the home corral.

The rapid beat
Of his broncho's feet
   On the sod as he speeds along,
Keeps living time
To the ringing rhyme
   Of his rollicking cowboy song.

One of the most famous of the cowboy songs is "The Old Chisholm Trail." It may interest you to notice—if you have not done so already—that this ballad almost sings itself. That is a very good sign that it is pure folklore—that is a production of the people. Every cowboy knows this song—many verses of it. When he had sung all the verses he *knew* he made up some more to suit himself; thus the song grew and grew without end. It is a song designed to be sung to the accompaniment of a horse in a jog trot.

The Old Chisholm Trail

Come along, boys, and listen to my tale,
I'll tell you of my troubles on the old Chisholm trail
   Coma ti yi youpy, youpy ya, youpy ya
   Coma ti yi youpy, youpy ya.

Oh, a ten-dollar hoss and a forty-dollar saddle,
And I'm goin' to punchin' Texas cattle.
  Coma ti yi youpy, etc.

I'm up in the mornin' afore daylight,
And afore I sleep the moon shines bright.

My hoss threwed me off in a creek called Mud,
My hoss threwed me off round the 2-U herd.

Last time I saw him he was going cross the level
A-kicking up his heels and a-running like the devil.

Oh, it's bacon and beans 'most every day—
I'd as soon be a-eatin' prairie hay.
  Coma ti yi youpy, youpy ya, youpy ya,
  Coma ti yi youpy, youpy ya.

The following verses, says Mr. Lomax, were used in many
parts of the West as a dance song. It is the farewell song of the
cowboy dance. When the party is ready to break up, this tune
is started, and all join in the singing while the fiddle remains
silent:

OLD PAINT

  Refrain:
  Good-bye, Old Paint, I'm a-leavin' Cheyenne,
  Good-bye, Old Paint, I'm a-leavin' Cheyenne.

  My foot in the stirrup, my pony won't stand;
  Good-bye, Old Paint, I'm a-leavin' Cheyenne.

  I'm riding Old Paint, I'm a-leadin' old Fab;
  Good-bye, Old Paint, I'm a-leavin' Cheyenne.

Mr. Lomax has gathered in this single volume more than 150
ballads such as the ones I have quoted. Everyone will find
something of interest among these ballads, and since they are
a part of the literature and the tradition of Texas, they should
be known by Texas boys and girls. The book is published by
the Macmillan Company, and sells, in the popular edition, for

75 cents. Mr. Lomax has a companion volume, *Songs of the Cattle Trail and Cow Camp,* that sells for $1.75. Of the two books, the first, *Cowboy Songs,* is the better.

I should be very glad to hear from any school that has set up a Texas Book Shelf in the school library. If either teachers or students would like to have this Texas Book Shelf write me, and perhaps I can suggest ways by which it can be provided.

(Editor's Note—Music has been arranged for a number of these cowboy songs by Oscar J. Fox, of San Antonio, a native Texan, born and bred in Burnet County and educated in music in the Municipal School of Music, Zurich, Switzerland, under Dr. Lothar Kempter and Dr. Carl Attenhofer. He returned to Texas in 1899 and has made his home since then in San Antonio. Although he has composed a number of art songs, it is his cowboy songs that have attracted attention to his work in all parts of this country. Carl Fischer, New York, has published the following for him: "Greer County," "Home on the Range," and "Rounded Up in Glory." G. Schirmer, New York, has published for him "The Cowboy's Lament," the song referred to above as "The Dying Cowboy." The Victor Company has recorded "Round Up in Glory." The record is Number 45387.)

P.S. The local history contest is now well under way. Hundreds of Texas boys and girls are busy gathering materials about the history of their communities. The contest will close May 1, but there is yet time for students to prepare essays. I will be glad to send the *History Teachers' Bulletin* to any student or teacher. Full directions are printed in this bulletin, as well as twenty of the best essays that were submitted last year. The prizes amount to $150.00. There are also prizes amounting to $150.00 for historical studies submitted by teachers.

VI ·

The Texas Bird Book

ALL DAY on Friday the boys of the Barnard High School might be seen conversing in small groups about the school building and on the athletic field. It was early spring before baseball practice had opened, and the boys were planning a long hike into the country. They were to go out on Friday night, camp at Cove Creek, and then continue the next day to Cisos Mountains that could be seen shimmering ten miles away to the west. The Cisos Mountains made the objective of all the hikes from the Barnard school. The boys liked to roam over the mountains, drink from the spring that gushed from under a cliff, and cook their meals over fires made of dry wood and enough green twigs to give the smoke of it a delightful tang. The mountains were full of small game and birds, and a week end out there brought the gang back feeling fit for work.

By dark on Friday night the gang of fifteen boys had reached Cove Creek, and they struck camp on the west side. Bill Robbins said that one should always cross a stream before making camp, as the stream might rise in the night and prevent crossing. Bill's grandfather had been a pioneer Texan, had ranched in the West and fought Indians, and knew much about the outdoors and the ways of nature. Bill had learned something of woodcraft from him. Bill's father was a businessman who con-

Interscholastic Leaguer, February, 1926.

fined himself to making money and playing golf. He did not
care much for outdoors or for nature, though he was glad to
provide for the interests of his son.

Bill was what the boys called a regular fellow. He took part
in athletics, but did not neglect his books. His greatest interest
was in a study of animals and birds. He had a sort of den in
the room over the garage, and had all sorts of collections there,
such as fossils, traps, old weapons, and books on nature subjects.

On Saturday morning the boys were cooking breakfast over
the campfire by sunup. It was a clear spring day, and the sun
rose with a brilliance that put everybody in a fine humor. While
the boys were getting ready to eat, "Slats" Hodge sang out:
"Say, fellers, what is that?" All the boys looked in the direction
Slats pointed, and saw a strange tiny bird flitting about in an
elm tree that stood on the bank of Cove Creek.

"Be quiet, fellows," said Bill Robbins, and the only motion
that followed was the curling up of the white smoke from the
campfire, and the only sound was the crackling of a green twig
on the fire. The boys noted that the bird's back was olive-
green, throat and chest black, and that the sides of the bird's
face were yellow. Its sides were streaked with white, and it had
black bars on the wings visible as the bird flitted about the
branches.

Then the little fellow began to sing the strangest notes:
zee-zee-zee-zee-zee. Then, as if he had seen enough, the bird
flitted rapidly away and took wing down Cove Creek.

"I guess he don't like our looks," said Slats.

"What kind of a bird is he?" asked Jim Dunnaway, turning
back to the bacon.

"He's a cheese bird," replied "Skinny" Langford, who always tried to be witty.

"Aw, lissen at Skinny!" said Slats in disgust.

"Well, boys," said Bill Robbins, "Skinny is not so far wrong.
The bird did sound as if he said 'Cheese, cheese—a little more
cheese.' "

Then the crowd realized that Skinny Langford might have had some reason for calling the bird a cheese bird.

"Naw," exclaimed "Shorty" Watkins, "he didn't say cheese. Whoever heard of a cheese bird? He said *'trees.' 'Trees, trees, murmuring trees.'* That's a tree bird."

By now all the boys were getting interested in what the little bird had said. They all wanted to know what sort of bird it was.

"Bill," said Slats, "tell this gang what kind of a bird that is."

"He's a green warbler, or green-throated warbler," said Bill. "Some call him the black-throated wood warbler."

"Good old Bill," and all the boys clapped.

This incident happening early in the morning got the boys interested in birds, and they found out that they did not know much about them. They knew crows, buzzards, hawks, mockingbirds, and English sparrows, but none of these save the mockingbird was very much worth knowing. When it came to the fine points of birds they knew nothing. Bill Robbins did not know all of them either, but he knew much more about them than the others.

They saw a bird that looked very much like a mockingbird, flew like a mockingbird, but had certain markings that indicated it was not. No one could tell what it was. Finally Bill told them that it was a butcher bird, or shrike. Then he gave them interesting information about this bloody bird. While it resembles a mockingbird, it has very different habits. It catches mice, small snakes, crickets, and even small birds. It has a strong beak and weak feet. Often when it catches a mouse or another bird it will fasten the dead victim to a barbed-wire fence or on a thorn of a tree. Because of this peculiar habit it is called a butcher bird. It has many other names, among which are French mockingbird, Spanish mockingbird, Indian mockingbird, grasshopper bird, and thornbird.

The boys found the birds plentiful that day, and heard many of them singing in anticipation of spring. They could not understand how it was that Bill Robbins knew so much more about birds than the others. Bill explained by saying that he studied birds, and read books on them. He would observe a bird, note its characteristics, and then look it up in the bird books.

The boys all agreed that they would take more interest in birds. "I wonder if they have any bird books in the school library?" said Jim Dunnaway.

"I tell you, boys," said Bill Robbins, "the best book on Texas birds has just come off the press. It is written by a University prof by the name of Simmons.⁴ It gives all you want to know about any Texas bird, and is, so far as I have been able to learn, the only book on Texas birds."

"How do you get that book?" asked Slats.

"It's published by the University of Texas. This man Simmons used to teach there, but he left to go on a trip to the South Seas to gather specimens of birds and animals for a museum."

"Gee, I'd like to take a trip like that," declared Gerren.

"Not only does this Simmons book tell about birds, but it gives the names of many Texas people who have been interested in birds, and has a page of their pictures. It has about everything you can imagine on birds. It tells where they live, how they build their nests, when they come and go, how they sing, and how they are marked. It's no trouble to learn about birds if you have that book."

"Why don't they get that book for the school library where all us fellows can see it? They've got a lot in there that I'd be willing to trade for this bird book. Let's ask Professor Jones to get us the bird book of Texas." This from Jim Dunnaway.

"Yes," said Slats, "Professor Jones is a good guy and knows what ought to be there, but he couldn't get that book unless he bought it himself. He'd have to go to the school board and ask for an appropriation."

"The school board is hard to get money out of," declared Skinny. "If we want that book, we'll have to buy it ourselves. I'm in favor of this gang buying that Texas bird book and put-

4. George Finlay Simmons, *Birds of the Austin Region.*

ting it in the library. I'll start it off. What does that book cost, Bill?"

"It costs $4."

"Well, I'll say it's worth it. We spend a lot of time learning things a thousand miles away, but Professor Jones says we ought to begin nearer home, and I'm thinking the same way."

And that is how the high school library at Barnard came to have George Finlay Simmons' Bird Book of Texas [*Birds of the Austin Region*], published by the University of Texas.

VII ·

The Life of Stephen F. Austin

"WHEN I AM DEAD justice will be done me." Thus wrote the founder and the father of Texas in what was to him the darkest hour of a life of sacrifice. He was at the time in a prison in Mexico, where he momentarily gave himself up to bitter reflections and despair.

"My situation," he said, "is desolate—almost destitute of friends and money, in a prison, amidst foes who are active to destroy me, and forgotten at home by those I faithfully labored to serve." Of his situation he asks what can be done "when Texas is silent as to me?"

Stephen F. Austin—Father of Texas!

For one hundred years—a whole century—Texas has been too silent as to you! But at last that long silence is broken, and in your own words, justice has been done you. Perhaps this silence has been too long, or perhaps it has taken Texas one hundred years to produce him who could do you full justice, who could set you forth in keeping with your work and service.

Stephen F. Austin, Father of Texas, gave to others but took nothing for himself. Here is his own description of his circumstances shortly before he died:

"I have no house, not a roof in all Texas that I can call my

Interscholastic Leaguer, April, 1926.

own. The only one I had was burned during the late invasion of the enemy. I make my home where the business of the country calls me. . . . I have no farm, no cotton plantation, no income, no money, no comforts. I have spent the prime of my life and worn out my constitution in trying to colonize this country. . . . My health and strength and time . . . have gone into the service of Texas, and I am therefore not ashamed of my present poverty." Yet in his poverty he could write: "The prosperity of Texas has been the object of my labors, the idol of my existence. It has assumed the character of a *religion,* for the guidance of my thoughts and actions, for fifteen years."

Stephen F. Austin! From the age of twenty-seven to forty-three he sacrificed all that men hold dear and desirable that Texas might live.

In the words of his biographer: "He was a man of warm affections, and loved the idea of home, but he never married. Texas was home and wife and family to him. He died on a pallet on the floor of a two-room clapboard shack, a month and twenty-four days past his forty-third birthday." And as he lay dying his thoughts were not of what life might have held for him, but of what was in store for the State he founded. Texas had gained her independence, but had not yet been recognized by the United States. "Texas recognized," he murmured. "Archer told me so. Did you see it in the papers?" That was all. He was dead. The time had come to do him justice.

The work of Stephen F. Austin, as set forth in Professor Eugene C. Barker's work, was too great to give here. At most I can only hope to touch some high spots, to show something of the dominant traits of the Man of Texas. Austin took up the work which his father had begun of colonizing the northern province of Mexico (Texas) with Anglo-Americans. He placed himself between two civilizations—one Latin and the other Teuton—and sought to harmonize them. The task proved impossible in the end, but it succeeded so far as the settlement of Texas went. For fifteen years he stood between the two races, the only man who understood both of them, and he sought to shield each from the blasts of the other. This made him appear at times to vacillate, to temporize, but always he had one object—the welfare of his colony. "I am operating," he said once in another connection, "on a pretty large scale for a taciturn and noiseless man, but I have no other object in view than the general prosperity of us all." On one occasion he advised his colonists in regard to an obnoxious Mexican law to "do as I have frequently been compelled to do—play the turtle, head and feet within your own shell. Some of the people may curse and abuse—no matter—they abused *me,* the best friend they ever had." Again, he said, "It has been my policy to slide along without any noise."

These quotations furnish the key to Austin's policy in Texas, a policy carried out with the highest degree of intelligence; they also accounted for his success. They further explain the fact that Austin never became a popular hero of the spectacular order. He is the real silent man of Texas, noiseless, but ever active, ever pushing forward his plans for Texas. He was past master of the indirect approach, and practiced it much on the Mexicans; but he could, when occasion demanded, be as direct as the bluntest American.

Until this book appeared practically nothing was known of Austin's personality. He has never been the subject of fireside stories, of legends such as have grown around the dominating personages of Sam Houston, Andrew Jackson, or Robert E. Lee. Austin had been too quiet, had "slid along without any noise." But in this book we find, doubtless, all that is to be known. Austin said little of religion, but thought a belief in religion "absolutely indispensable for the wellbeing and sound organization of all societies." He had little use for lawyers, and thought they stirred up ill feeling and litigation. He read books on politics, economics, diplomacy, law, history, and novels. He lived plainly on simple food and insisted that members of his family live simply and dress in homespun and cotton out of regard for the poor people of the colony. He had evolved a philosophy of life which taught him that the world was what one made it. "All trouble or not so bad"; that a puncheon-floored hut or an Indian camp was sufficient when a better house and life were in prospect—and to Austin these were always in prospect. At one time he went far above all his settlements and selected the site he would have for his home. It commanded a splendid view of the Colorado River, of the purple hills and the green valleys. Doubtless, in Austin's imagination (this is the reviewer talking now) he pictured himself setting up a home and a capital comparable with Mt. Vernon and Washington. The home was never built, though plans were drawn, but the State capitol and the State university stand on the site selected by Austin, and Austin's remains lie in the State Cemetery there among the heroes of Texas.

As hinted before, this book contains all that is known of Stephen F. Austin. A word as to the author and the book.

Dr. Eugene C. Barker, professor of American history at the University of Texas, is the author of the book. For twenty years he devoted his spare time to research which would enable him to set forth with accuracy and precision the life and labors of the Father of Texas. In that time he tracked Austin as a detective trails a criminal—in fact, the historian is but a detective of the past, and his methods of research bear a striking resemblance to a detective's methods of investigation. The historian followed his man from Missouri to Texas, to Mexico, back to Texas, then to prison in Mexico, through the early days of the Revolution, and then to the United States and back to Texas to stand by the pallet on which Austin died. Not only did he follow, but he has left the record of his work. There are blind trails, gropings with insufficient evidence, but each time the reader is apprised of success or failure, and the degree thereof. This the scholar owes to posterity—to put all his resources, all his sources—regardless of what they cost him—before the world in order that others may reap the knowledge thus sown.

Dr. Barker has met the obligation fully, but without that display that makes one too conscious of the scholarship. It is an integral part of the whole.

The style of the book exhibits the impeccable taste shown in the scholarship. The language is the vehicle of thought, and attains that fine distinction of a style that all but escapes notice. Occasionally a sentence moves with such swiftness and incisiveness as to attract attention. These sentences, lifted from their context, would lose their force; but one may be permitted. The author is describing the machinations and schemes of those trying to discredit Austin in Mexico at the time he went there on his unfortunate mission of 1832.

"And weaving in and out of the background (of chicanery and misrepresentation) was Colonel Anthony Butler, grasping at straws and plotting incessantly for the transfer of Texas to the United States, to the accomplishment of which he considered Austin the most serious obstacle."

Andrew Jackson surpassed Professor Barker in brevity of description when he wrote on the back of one of Butler's proposals "A. Butler—scoundrel"; but Barker not only gave Butler's character but his method as well, all in one sentence, if not in the first happily chosen word.

It would be a great book that had no fault for a reviewer to find. In the preface Professor Barker tells us that little was written about Austin, and that he has never been the subject of a biographical study. "It is in what he (Austin) did and the manner of doing it that the admirable character and winning personality of the man must appear." Without doubt both of these do appear, and in a form that would be pleasing to Austin and at the same time not displeasing to Austin's enemy. Yet nowhere has Professor Barker given a description of Austin's appearance, height, color of hair, complexion, or manner. It would have been an addition. We know how he felt and acted—how he would act under given conditions; we would like to know more of his personal appearance than is revealed in his portraits. But even so, this biography has made Austin's prophecy—"When I am dead justice will be done me"—come true.

Appropriately enough, the book is a Texas product from start to finish. It is issued by the Cokesbury Press, of Dallas, is illustrated with photographs, drawings, and maps, and is fully indexed. The book sells for $5.

66

VIII ·

Fulmore's *History*

THERE HAS not been published in Texas a more unique book than Fulmore's *History and Geography of Texas as Told in County Names*. The book was first published by Judge Z. T. Fulmore in 1915, and it has now been revised and republished by the author's son, Sterling R. Fulmore.

As the title indicates, the book deals with the county names of Texas. Regardless of what county you may live in, you can find in this little volume about all that is known of the origin of the county name. Angelina County means "little angel," and the name is derived from the Angelina River. La Salle County is named for the immortal Frenchman; Travis, Crockett, Fannin, Burleson, and scores of others were called after Texas heroes. Colorado means "red water," Blanco means "white," Brazos signifies "branch" or "arm," Concho is the Spanish word for "shell," El Paso signifies "the pass." Delta County is so called because it is shaped like the Greek letter Delta. And so on for the 253[5] counties of the State.

With the emphasis that is now being placed on county history, this republication of Fulmore's valuable book is very timely. The book makes a starting point for the history of every county in Texas. Another valuable feature is a table showing

Interscholastic Leaguer, September, 1926.
5. Crane County was not organized until 1927.

the derivation of every county in Texas. For example, the old eastern counties were parent counties and the western ones were carved from their territory. From Bexar County, or municipality, more than 120 counties have been formed. In old days Bexar extended to the Rio Grande and El Paso. Other parent counties are Bastrop, Milam, Gonzales, Red River, San Patricio, and Washington. In the appendix of the book appear some of the important treaties affecting the history of Texas.

This volume makes an indispensable reference book for all libraries. Newspaper editors, authors, teachers, and students will find it interesting and useful. Everyone will find in it something of interest because there is in it something concerning every community.

Many schools are building up in their libraries what is known as the Texas Book Shelf. It is a good move. All the books in print on Texas could be put on a shelf less than five feet wide. All the books worth having that are in print could go on a smaller space. There should be a Texas Book Shelf in your school and Fulmore's history should be on it. The book may be had from S. R. Fulmore at Austin. The price is $2.50.

IX ·

Texas Folk-Lore, Volume V

> Froggie went courting, and he did ride,
>> Uhn-huhn
> Froggie went courting, and he did ride,
> A sword and pistol by his side,
>> Uhn-huhn
> He stopped at Mistress Mousie's door
> And aloud he did roar.
>
> Where shall the wedding supper be?
> Way down yonder in the hollow tree.
> First came in was a bumblebee,
> And he tuned his fiddle on his knee.
> Next came in was Captain Tick,
> And he et so much it made him sick.

HERE IN THE NEW volume of the Texas Folk-Lore Society is the complete story of that old song, "The Frog's Courting," that has brought much joy to childhood wherever the English language is spoken. For centuries boys and girls have thrilled in imagining Mr. Frog going out courtin', and have gone vicariously through many adventures until he was stopped by

This is Texas Folk-Lore Society Publication V, reviewed in *Interscholastic Leaguer,* November, 1926.

the old gray cat or swallowed up by a big black snake, according to the version of the song.

Dr. L. W. Payne has presented to the lovers of folk tales a rare treat in his article on "Frog's Courtin'." I have been so interested in reading his many versions that I have not had time to count them. Therefore I cannot tell you how many there are. I can assure you that the song as you know it, or have known it, is there. The wedding supper was certainly one grand feast for all the animals.

> What shall we have for the wedding supper?
> Black-eyed peas and bread and butter.
> Next came in was Colonel Flea,
> And danced the jig with the bumblebee.
> The next to appear was old Sis cow,
> Who tried to dance but didn't know how.

Dr. Payne has collected versions of his song from all parts of Texas, and has found that the song came into Texas from practically all of the older states. But I dare say that most readers will be more interested in the songs themselves.

If you feel that these old songs have lost their charm, take them home and read them to any member of the family. To the older ones they will recall happy childhood memories; to the children they will bring the delight that has caused them to live for so many centuries that no one knows whence they came.

This "Frog Courting Song" is but one of the many delights to be found in J. Frank Dobie's new volume of folklore that is just off the press. This is the fifth volume issued by the Texas Folk-Lore Society, and while it is not the best volume, it has in it many excellent things. Mrs. Mattie Austin Hatcher gives us a Texas border ballad, which Spanish students can try their teeth on, since it is written in Spanish. John K. Strecker has gathered together all the lore about snakes, toads, and lizards. In it you can find out all about hoop snakes, jointed snakes, how snakes swallow their young and go blind when they shed

their skins. If you cannot really find out about all these things, you can learn what people think about them, which is often more interesting than the facts themselves.

Mary Jourdan Atkinson has passed many hour bringing together the familiar sayings of old-time Texans. In truth, the sayings are familiar to Texans, but they are also familiar to practically all of America.

J. Frank Dobie has an article on the Tournament. This is not folklore, but a clear description and exposition of a social custom. Of the same nature is Branch Isbell's story of early Texas dances, and Mary Daggett Lake's presentation of Tarrant County Christmas customs. E. R. Bogusch has an extensive collection of Bexar County superstitions, and Douglas Branch has a documented article on the buffalo.

Professor R. C. Harrison, of the Texas Tech faculty, and Professor Gates Thomas, of the San Marcos State Teachers' College faculty, present contributions on the Negro folklore. Professor Harrison undertakes to show that the Negro has become his own interpreter of his folklore, and that his interpretation is to be found in his spirituals, or religious songs. Professor Thomas gives us the songs themselves. The two English professors would, I dare say, have a hard time coming to any agreement as to what the Negro folk songs mean. Professor Harrison seems to find that the Negro's songs indicate that the black man is slowly working his way out to a lofty plane of poetic and spiritual expression. Professor Thomas does not state just what he thinks about it all. He merely sets down the songs that he has heard since 1885, and he has them arranged in chronological order. The songs speak for themselves and for their composers.

The first one is pretty bad, and they appear to get worse and worse until they are barely fit to print. If Professor Harrison had used Professor Thomas' material he would have been forced to different conclusions. But perhaps he could have come out even by stating that many of the songs quoted by Professor

Thomas did not originate with the Negro, but with the white men, and were sung by them as much as, if not more than, by Negroes. Should he say that, there are some who would agree with him.

There is something in this last volume of folklore that will interest everyone. The material in it comes from the Texas soil, and it has all the variety and raciness of that soil. The book has 190 pages and sells for $1.25.

X ·

A Ranchman's Recollections

WHEN I STARTED writing these talks on Texas books I
thought I was a free moral agent, and that I could do it if I
wanted to and stop when I got ready. But it seems that I calculated without my editor. The editor is, on the whole, a good
sort of a fellow. But he has come to the point that he seems to
think I am hired to him and not to the State of Texas. He calls
me up now and demands that I send him a book talk every
month. The fact that books on Texas are getting scarce or that
I may be busy with my own affairs troubles him not at all. I am
convinced that if I could find no new book on Texas, he
would expect me to write one in order that I might have something to talk about in this column. I do like to read Texas
books, talk about them, and if I have time, write about them,
but I do not want this editor to take the position that I have to
do it unless he can see his way clear to raise my pay. He seems
inclined to ride a free horse too hard. W. P. W.

THIS BOOK was written by the late Mr. Frank S. Hastings,
manager for several years of the Swenson Ranch near Stam-
ford, in what he calls "the big pasture country." It is little

Interscholastic Leaguer, January, 1927.

known except among the cattlemen. There are in the book many things of peculiar interest to Texas people. It was in Texas that the cattle industry was born and flourished. The first effort to ship beef in refrigerator cars was made, according to Mr. Hastings, at Denison, Texas, about 1874. The experiment was a failure because the cars could not be re-iced between Denison and Kansas City, or St. Louis, and the meat spoiled. The first chilled meat that was shipped was in barrels. A joint of stovepipe would be put down in the center of the barrel and filled with ice. Today mechanical refrigeration is used on cars, and ice is unnecessary.

Mr. Hastings tells about the captains of the meat packing industry, G. F. Swift and Phillip D. Armour. Both men started life in humble circumstances, and in the rapid development of America following the Civil War built up great industries and fortunes.

There is hardly a cattleman or a man connected with the beef industry that Mr. Hastings did not know personally. He mentions Andy Adams and George W. Saunders as authorities on the cattle drive; he describes cowboys, cow horses, and life on the range. On the cow horse he quotes from Brininstool:

THE OLD COW HOSS

No, he ain't so much fer beauty, fer he's scrubby
    an' he's rough.
An' his temper's sort o'sassy, but you bet
    he's good enough!
Fer he'll take the trail o'mornings
    be it up or be it down,
On the range a huntin' cattle or a
    lopin' into town,
An' he'll leave the miles behind him
    and he'll never sweat a hair,
'Cuz he is a willing critter when he's
    goin' anywhere.

> Oh, your thoroughbred at runnin'
>   in a race may be the boss
> But fer all-day ridin' lemme have the
>   Ol' Cow Hoss.

Mr. Hastings has placed us all in his debt by saving some of the ranch stories. As storytellers the western pioneers have never been surpassed. They had the knack of giving to a story an elemental dramatic force that ordinarily is exercised by those highly talented. Most of the stories are those told to Mr. Hastings by Mage, one of the SMS men. I give one paragraph from the story entitled "The Storm."

"We hadn't much more'n got to the herd when the air freshened an' things begin to git right. Then it got cold, and we could hear it coming. Thunder and lightnin' seemed to spring out of the mesquites. The foreman passed the word: 'Hold 'em till they git wet,' an' we begin to circle. The cattle was on their feet in a second, with the first cold air, but we got the mill started by the time the storm hit. I've seen lightnin', but thet was lightnin' right. As far as thet's consarn, I've seen balls o' fire on the end of a steer's horn many a time, but there was a ball o' fire on both horns of every one o' them thousin' steers, an' the light in the balls of their eyes looked like two thousin' more. Talk about a monkey wrench fallin' from a windmill an' givin' you a sight o' the stars, or one of them Andy Jackson fireworks clubs puttin' off Roman candles at a Fort Worth parade! They're jest sensations; this here show I'm tellin' you about was real experience. We seen things."

There is another story called "Ol' Grand Pa," a horse story, the story of a race. I wanted to publish one of these stories, but the editor said he did not have room for it. I think they are the best stories I have ever read, even if they were told by Mage, the cowboy on the SMS Ranch.

The book is published by the *Breeders' Gazette,* 542 South Dearborn Street, Chicago, Ill.

(Editor's Note. Mr. Webb is getting discouraged. He tells me that schools generally are not interested in his Texas Book Shelf idea. We believe they are and we want to convince him. Won't those schools which have ordered any of the Texas books he has recommended in his column write the *Leaguer* a note so advising?)

XI ·

History Teachers' Bulletin, Volume XIV, Number 1

THE UNIVERSITY PRESS has just published the *History Teachers' Bulletin* which contains the twenty or more essays that took prizes or received special mention in the last Caldwell local history contest. These essays were written by the school boys and girls of Texas, and many of them have genuine historical interest and value.

The first prize was won by Grace Lowe Butler of San Antonio. Her essay bears the title, "General John Lapham Bullis: The Friend of the Frontier." General Bullis was a soldier and Indian fighter stationed in Texas in the period following the Civil War; his business was to protect the frontier from the Indians. At one time he had in his command the famous Seminole scouts, Indians who acted as trailers and scouts for the white men.

The second prize went to Albert Cranz of Beaumont. His subject was the origin and history of the Spindletop oil field. Spindletop was the first great oil field in Texas, though not the oldest. This story is extremely interesting and, in addition, is a valuable contribution. The history of the oil industry in Texas is one that should challenge a good historian.

The most unusual contribution came from the Rio Grande Valley. It is the history of the shortest railroad in the United

Interscholastic Leaguer, February, 1928.

States, one of the antiques of American civilization. The essay was written by Anna Cora Petz, of Brownsville. Here is a description of how water was provided for the little engine:

"A Brownsville photographer went to Point Isabel for the purpose of doing some photographic work there. The train stopped at a small midway station. The photographer, after waiting for a long time, began to grow impatient and got down to see what the trouble was. What he saw was a situation which struck him as exceedingly funny. A gang-plank had been stretched from the water-tank to the engine. Across this plank a number of Mexicans were carrying pails of water to the engine. He took a picture of the scene and found a ready sale for it in the Valley, whence it was broadcasted later in the form of postcards. The management of the railroad, however, failed to see the humor of the situation."

Soon after this occurred the little engine was discarded for a gasoline engine.

In another essay from Tyler we find a price list of goods in 1870. It ran like this:

Shoes—$2.25	$2.25
4 yd flannel	1.60
One qt whiskey	1.00
1 pair boots	6.50
5½ yds jeans	5.50

Then there is the story of Galveston Island and of Jean Lafitte, of Fort Phantom Hill, of some Ante-Bellum teachers of San Antonio, and of the Old Stone Fort at Nacogdoches. Every part of the State is represented. The work was done by high school boys and girls under the direction of their history and English teachers.

At the end of the book is the account of the American Revolutionary soldiers buried in Texas. An investigation was begun some two years ago to determine whether any Revolutionary soldiers were buried in Texas. The investigators found five and perhaps seven.

This bulletin containing all these essays, together with the rules and regulations for the contest which ends in May, will be sent free upon request to teachers, history students, and newspaper editors. All are invited to read and make use of this material and it is hoped that a great many will enter the contests for this year for prizes totaling $150. Address requests to W. P. Webb, University Station, Austin, Texas.

XII ·

Texas Wild Flowers

FOR THREE YEARS now I have been writing for the *Interscholastic Leaguer* short talks on Texas books. I have tried to select only those books that pertained to Texas, and those that I thought would be or should be of particular interest to the school boys and girls and to those who teach them. In these little articles I have told of books about the cattle trails and ranching by Andy Adams, George W. Saunders, and Frank S. Hastings, about folklore by J. Frank Dobie and other Texas writers, and about birds by George Finlay Simmons. These authors are well known, and most of them are becoming more famous through their writings. All of them love Texas, and have put a part of their love into their works. Their books have grown, so to speak, out of the soil of Texas, and are the beginnings of a literature and a culture that is very promising for the future.

I have written these articles because I thought the boys and girls of Texas, and their teachers too, would like to know about our own State. It is easy for us to come to think that all the interesting things are in far-off countries—the farther off the better. But if we would read of our own State we could learn that Texas is among the most charming places in all the world. I dare say that a New England boy would look upon a trip to

Interscholastic Leaguer, November, 1928.

Texas as an adventure which he would want to tell to all his friends throughout the school year.

I have written of these books because I thought that the teachers would like to set up in the school libraries a special shelf for Texas books, and buy the good ones as they fall from the press to add to the old ones. I believed that the school boards and the parents would be willing to furnish the money to buy the books for this Texas Book Shelf in order that their boys and girls might know something about the State in which we live and which we all love so dearly. I know that some schools have set up a Texas Book Shelf because the teachers have told me about it. I hope that other teachers will do the same. It is a good thing to do because the boys and girls who are in school today must be the authors and writers of tomorrow. If any books are to be written about Texas twenty or thirty years from now, the work must be done by those who are now in the public schools. It is only by knowing Texas that we can write about it, and the Texas Book Shelf offers us the best opportunity to gain this knowledge.

Mr. Bedichek and I have talked many times about the Texas Book Shelf. Once I expressed to him some doubt as to whether or not any books on Texas were being bought as a result of these talks. He thought that books were being bought and others would be bought. I think he wanted me to continue to write the articles to help fill up his columns so he would not have so much to do himself. He is that way. Well, he made a statement. I do not remember exactly what he said, but it was to the effect that he would be willing to give each year a prize to the school library that first reported the establishment of a Texas Book Shelf with as many as ten volumes. The prize would be given for the best essay written by a student on the way in which the Texas Book Shelf was established. The prize to go, I believe, not to the pupil but to the school library. It may be that Mr. Bedichek has changed his mind or spent the money he proposed to spend in some other way. I leave that to him.

The reason I am continuing the column is that a new book

has just appeared that is so different from anything that came before it that I cannot resist the temptation to tell you about it. It differs from the other books in three ways: It was written by a teacher in the public schools, it was written by a woman, and it was written about Texas flowers.

Most of the books I have talked about were written either by college professors or cowboys, or by a mixture of the two. Ordinarily public schoolteachers do not have time to write books. When they are not busy teaching, they are looking after the investment of the money that comes from the large salaries paid them by school boards and, consequently, do not turn often to scholarship and authorship. Therefore, the appearance of a book by a teacher, or by one who until recently was a teacher in the public schools, is an event that causes wonder, admiration, and applause.

This particular book was written by a woman, and, as I said above, all the others I mention have been written by college professors and cowboys. The reason I have waited so long to take notice of a book by a woman is due solely to the fact that the women have waited so long to write one. While the women have been teaching school, the college professors and cowboys have been neglecting their main jobs to write books. But now the women have taken over all the schoolteaching jobs and have started in on authorship. If they are as successful in that as they have been in teaching, then most of the books from now on will be by women.

In the third place, this book is about flowers—the flowers of Texas, beautiful, fragrant, blossoming flowers. In it we meet our old friends of the field and stream, the humble little flower that first appears in spring, the flamboyant firewheel of mid-summer, bluebells and buckthorn, milkweed and catclaw, sweet William and Virginia creeper, soapweed and sunflower, honey-bloom and hedgehog cactus, and a thousand others that we see day by day without recognizing half of them.

Did you ever stop to think how ignorant we are of the things around us? We go to school nine months in the year to learn

83

Texas Wild Flowers

cial use. Of our old friend the sunflower she tells us many strange things: that it was cultivated by the Hurons, thread was made from its fiber, fodder from its leaves, dye from its petals, and hair tonic and food from its seeds. The fiber is used in China to adulterate silk, the seeds are fed to parrots in the United States, and in Russia they are peddled on the streets as are peanuts. The oil is used to make soap, candles, and salad dressing, and the stems for paper. Any Texas boy can add that they infest peach orchards, dull hoes, and furnish a home for countless thousands of chiggers who are never loath to leave it. Since the author was never a boy, she could not know these things. That is about the only fault I can find with her book.

It would be a shame to put this book on a book shelf, even a Texas Book Shelf. It would cause too much trouble and too many arguments over whose turn it was to have it. Each individual, certainly each family, ought to have a copy. The Boy Scouts and Girl Scouts of Texas ought to adopt it as a handbook to take on every excursion into the country. It is a good gift for birthdays and for Christmas, one that is different and that can but be appreciated. It is and will become a part of the culture of Texas, and a thorough knowledge of it will go far toward marking one who has it as a cultivated person. This brings me to another serious fault I have to find with the book. It was written too late. It should have been written when I was a small boy roaming the fields and prairies of West Texas. But at that time women were not writing books, and this book was best done by a woman.

Ellen D. Schulz, *Texas Wild Flowers,* Laidlow Bros., Chicago.

XIII ·

Texas Literature

THERE HAS JUST come from the press a little volume by
Dr. L. W. Payne, of the English Department of the University
of Texas, entitled *A Survey of Texas Literature*. The book, or
pamphlet, is what its title indicates. Dr. Payne has undertaken
to examine the books that have been written about Texas or
by Texas people, and to appraise their literary value. The first
part of the book is devoted to the literary output of Texas from
the time of Cabeza de Vaca to the end of the Civil War. In
this period there was a beginning of history, fiction, and poetry.
Although the history and the fiction of the time have been surpassed by later writers, it seems to be generally agreed that the
best poetry produced in or about Texas to date was written at
this time. Mirabeau B. Lamar's "The Daughter of Mendoza"
and Reuben M. Potter's "Hymn of the Alamo" seem to hold
first rank in poetry.

The outstanding development after the Civil War was the
rise of literature, history, fiction, and poetry, about the cattle
country and the cowboy. And of this that which will probably
endure longest is the cowboy ballad, folk song. Dr. Payne mentions more or less briefly all who have done any considerable
writing about the cattle country. He calls the period in which
this writing appeared the transition period. In the section de-

voted to the more recent period, one finds the names of Texas writers still living. Among them are Dorothy Scarborough, Barry Benefield, John W. Thomason, Jr., Ruth Cross, George Patullo, Karle Wilson Baker, Clyde Hill, Grace Noll Crowell, John P. Sjolander, Larry Chittenden, Leonard Doughty, Stark Young, and that beloved genius whose name was William Sidney Porter, known to us as O. Henry. In conclusion, Dr. Payne gives some attention to the various agencies, newspapers, book reviews, clubs, and libraries that have promoted an interest in Texas art and literature.

This volume devoted to a survey of Texas literature is a good sign. It means, in the first place, that the history of this State is now sufficiently long to justify a book about Texas books. It means that art and literature are on the way. In the second place, the fact that a reputable publisher was willing to go to the expense of bringing out this book is almost a sure sign that there is among the people a present or potential demand for such a work.

It is quite fitting, too, that Dr. Payne, of the English Department of the University of Texas, should have prepared such a volume. The hundreds of teachers in this State who have studied under him realize that he is well fitted by training and by inclination to do something for Texas in this way. In that respect Dr. Payne is unique, with possibly one or two exceptions. Dr. Payne is not only interested in the books he wrote about— or the book he wrote—but he is interested in the people who wrote them. Perhaps no one requires sympathy born of understanding more than one who writes. It must have been some such character as Dr. Payne that Stark Young had in mind when he wrote recently in *The New Republic:*

"I am thinking of P————'s generous interest and concern long ago when I was writing my first lines, of that unending assurance that he wanted me to turn out well, write beautifully, and that art was a natural impulse, not a luxury. . . . This great gift of creative generosity and warmth of heart that he has, enables him to see this man (the author) as the man himself wishes to be seen. . . . He wishes for you your own kind of perfection, and senses your desire and motion toward it. He becomes your best public because more and more of you goes where more and more of you is welcome; and your best critic because he helps you to judge what you have done, not by the achievement of others, but by what is possible to you."

Stark Young's characterization, which suits Dr. Payne to a T, indicates unmistakably a person well qualified to do just what Dr. Payne has done. Those Texas authors whose names are mentioned in this volume may be thankful that Dr. Payne understands men as well as books.

Dr. Payne's book brings up the question: Does Texas really have a literature? Many people, supposedly well informed, deny that it has; they say the State is too young, its culture too immature. That would seem to be the opinion of some of the great universities of this State and, therefore, of the controlling members of their faculties. So far as I know there is not a course in English in any State-supported institution in Texas that devotes more than casual notice to Texas literature. And some have refused outright to permit such a course to be given.

It would seem that the public schools of this State have an opportunity to take the lead in the study of Texas literature. Dr. Payne's contribution has made that possible. In time, it may be, the universities and colleges will follow the example and make some provision for a study of the artistic and literary efforts native to the soil that supports them.

L. W. Payne, *A Survey of Texas Literature,* Rand McNally & Co., Chicago. 50 cents.

XV ·

The Book of Texas

Review by L. W. PAYNE, JR.

WITHOUT INTRODUCTORY fanfare or self-laudatory advertisement *The Book of Texas,* Volume XXI of *The Book of Knowledge* published by the Grolier Society of New York, has just been issued under the imprint of the Dallas office of the Society, copyright 1929. It is a book which has been edited with considerable care, and there is here accumulated a vast amount of information about the State, its history, its resources, its industries, its cities, its flora and fauna, its schools and colleges, its religious and social life, its literature and art, its song and legend and story.

Among the contributors are a number of distinguished Texas educators, though the editors for some unaccountable reason have failed to identify the contributions of the respective authors. Dr. Holland Thompson, professor of history in the College of the City of New York and lecturer in Columbia University, is the general editor, and Dr. Charles W. Ramsdell of the University of Texas, is the general adviser on the volume. Among the contributors are the following: Professor Walter P. Webb (accidentally printed William P. Webb in the list of contributors) of the University of Texas, who writes the opening

Interscholastic Leaguer, October, 1929.

article on the history of Texas under the title "The Lone Star State"; Professor J. Frank Dobie, who writes on "Literature and Art in Texas"; Professor Annie Webb Blanton of the University of Texas, who writes on "Public Education in Texas." The contributions of the remaining writers we are unable to identify positively, but we judge that Professor John H. McGinnis of Southern Methodist University is responsible for the article on "Colleges and Universities"; Miss Harriet Smith of Sam Houston State Teachers College on the geography of Texas under the title "The Empire We Call Texas"; Dr. S. D. Warner of Sam Houston State Teachers College on "The Wild Life in Texas"; Professor W. R. Banks of Prairie View State Normal on "The Negro in Texas"; and Allen Chaffee, author of "Linda's El Dorado" and other pioneer stories, and W. A. Stephenson of the department of history and government in Simmons University, whose contributions we are unable to identify.

The historical survey by Professor Webb is an interesting and well-written condensation of the whole of the romantic history of Texas under her six flags. The article on Texas literature, art, sculpture, and music by Professor Dobie is a pioneer effort in this direction and is well worthy of close reading. The articles by Miss Blanton and Professor McGinnis are dependable and instructive, and the other articles seem equally authoritative.

The book is profusely illustrated and attractive in its format. The index of sixteen double-column pages adds distinctively to the usefulness of the volume as a reference book.

XIX ·

The Great Plains, by Walter Prescott Webb

Review by ROY BEDICHEK

READERS OF the *Leaguer* have long been familiar with the name of the author of this volume. It was his idea that every book of especial significance to Texas life and history should be accounted for in this paper under the caption "Talks on Texas Books." He originated this column and has been the most frequent contributor to it. It was his suggestion, also, that the school library institute a Texas Book Shelf, whereon Texas books be grouped together.

History, Mr. Webb believes, should stand on its own ground, so to speak. For several years he conducted through the columns of the *Leaguer* a local history contest, stimulating school children to study their own environments on the theory that in history, as in other departments of knowledge, the Socratic "Know Thyself" is of first importance. As teacher of history in the University of Texas for the past fifteen years, he has inspired many students to turn their attention to local history with excellent results. Future historians will be grateful for this record.

The father of Texas history (at least, in so far as serious scientific work is concerned) was Professor George P. Garri-

Interscholastic Leaguer, January, 1932.

son, for whom the social science building at the University is named. He was succeeded by Dr. Eugene C. Barker, his protégé and disciple, who has given the major portion of his time to Texas history, to the end that the early work of our pioneers has been better and more authentically recorded than that of any other American pioneer group except, perhaps, those of the original thirteen colonies. Dr. Herbert E. Bolton, although not a native, readily caught up an enthusiasm for Texas history; and, during his few years in this State, he did notable research in Spanish-American history in its relation to the Southwest, a field now being enriched by the work of Dr. Charles W. Hackett. In the same enterprising department, Dr. Charles W. Ramsdell has specialized for years in the history of the southern states, articulating Texas history with that important contact. The author of the present volume, one of the younger men of the department, has turned his face to the west, connecting up Texas history with the development of the regions lying to the west and north.

No school library of Western Texas or of the Middle West can do without a copy (better, several copies) of this book. The civics teacher cannot afford to be without it, for it explains for the first time (in available form) the genesis of many of the civic peculiarities of the communities of this great area. The history teacher must have it as a reference guide, for, though it is not history in the usual acceptation of the term, it makes the development of the Great Plains clear in large outline, leaving to the usual school history the task of merely filling in details. The English teacher (more than any other) needs this book in order to arouse in pupils a realization of their own environment, so that they may write with intelligence and inspiration of the life which they find around them. Certainly the teacher of geography will find in it the kind of treatment which alone gives that subject any significance, namely, the influence of geography upon human thought and ways and institutions.

Although recommended for use in the schoolroom, the book is by no means dull, as the term "schoolbook" unfortunately implies. The general reader finds here the record of an episode in the march of machine civilization. Of course, economists, as a class, are more interested in machine civilization than are historians. The economist has described its workings in England and in Western Europe. The United States, being the foremost industrialized nation in the world, has not been neglected. He has also recorded its cancerous work among the backward peoples and the revolution it wrought in congested Japan. He keeps industriously on the trail of what it is doing now in Russia, and so on; but it remained for Mr. Webb to discover and describe, right under the nose of the American economist, the behavior of machine civilization when it came upon a vast, isolated, and practically unoccupied area. The conquest of the Great Plains, as told in this book, has the aspect of a record of a laboratory experiment. The essential conditions appear to have been fixed, set up, and arranged with the necessary precision for exact demonstration. Moreover, Professor Webb tells it with the dramatic foreshortening of a well-conceived play. The experiment itself proceeds with rapidity and is all accomplished in a unit of time short enough to offer no difficulty to the un-historical imagination. It is, therefore, a not unimportant contribution to the great mass of literature which has grown up in response to our eagerness to understand just what the industrial revolution has done and is now doing to us.

The author uses three tests for delimiting the area which he proposes to treat: (1) treelessness; (2) semi-aridity; (3) level surface. Applying these tests one after another, the reader finds a great central region of America satisfying them. This section, then, is called "The High Plains." The region eastward (approximately set off by the 98th meridian) satisfying only two of the tests, is named "The Prairie Plains," while certain areas west of "The High Plains," really mountainous plateaus, are included with the other two sections under the designation, "Great Plains Environment."

A western bartender once queried a hilarious cowboy who was "roughhousing" the saloon, "Looky here, aint you coverin' too much territory?" The same rhetorical question might have been with some reason put to the author of the present volume as he was writing the second paragraph of page 7. The unity of the work is impaired by this stretching of one hand to the southern shore of Lake Michigan while the other is toying with the lock on the Golden Gate. It is beyond even Mr. Webb's clever hand to make Nevada and Illinois lie down together and behave properly as units bound together in the same environmental sheaf. The ambitious incisors disengage a larger portion than the historical molars can properly masticate. But more of this later.

The old school histories usually begin with "Our ancestors emerged from the forests of Germany." Forests imply humidity, and, in northern latitudes, suggest also a broken, if not mountainous country. So, the people who occupied the eastern portion of the United States in the beginning of the nineteenth century found themselves in a broken-humid-forested environment; and their folkways, institutions, and technique of pioneering had been formed for many generations in this kind of country. The industrial revolution had just gotten well-set in America when the pressure of population made the demand for land imperious. The rigors of Canadian climate to the north and the hostile Spanish-American setup to the south, turned the mainstream of pioneer migration due west.

"Then," says the author, ". . . they crossed the Mississippi and came out on the Great Plains, an environment with which they had had no experience. The result was a complete though temporary breakdown of the machinery and ways of pioneering. They began to make adjustments, and this book is the story of those adjustments . . . ways of life and living changed."

Substitute in the above paragraph "High Plains" for "Great Plains" and that part of the book which adheres firmly to this thesis is indeed excellent.

What are some of the things that come within the purview of the historian of the High Plains who adopts this institutional rather than the more conventional method? In the first place, it develops a charming essay on the six-shooter. The author shows that the conquest of the Plains Indian would have been practically impossible without it. The invention came from a Connecticut Yankee named Colt, and its manufacture on a large scale was possible only by an industrialized community. This is followed by the best chapter in the book, "The Cattle Kingdom." The fencing problem was met with the invention and manufacture on a large scale of barbed wire, and the barbed-wire industry is given ample treatment. The windmill, or rather the American adaptation of the windmill, is the subject of another section. Thus link by link the author ties the conquest of the High Plains to the business of manufacturing. Dry farming is treated as a method of culture developed there requiring appropriate tools, and so on. The work goes astray in its treatment of irrigation, for the true plains are not nor can they ever be irrigated, and by the same token, the elaborate treatment of the windmill, the six-shooter, the barbed-wire fence, dry farming, irrigation are all beside the point in most of the area which the author includes in the "Great Plains Environment" east of the 98th meridian. If a history of irrigation is necessary, because the area to be treated includes some of the Rocky Mountain states so would a history of mining be. In short, the book's reach exceeds its grasp in this particular.

That portion which deals with irrigation, irrigation laws, the "Literature," and "Mysteries" of the Great Plains should appear as appendices, or better still as separate monographs. If a New York dude with a fair proficiency in turning off newspaper verse may figure in the "Literature of the Great Plains," then Dvorák, visiting Bohemian kin in the edge of the Plains environment and gathering material for writing his "New World Symphony," should be included in a chapter on the "Music of the Great Plains"; and certainly there should be built around Remington a chapter on the "Pictures of the Great Plains"; and another chapter is necessary on the "Sculpture of the Great Plains" since Gutzon Borglum is carving historical faces on some cliff in the Black Hills; and so on. The roots of art and religion go too deep to require more than casual mention in such a book.

Judged from a purely literary standpoint, the hostile and diligent critic might find some fairly juicy pickings. There are chapters of first-rate exposition; incidents are told with a gusto that betrays the natural-born storyteller; there are dashes of humor, and philosophical asides which are stimulating. On the other hand, there are occasional faults of diction or imagery, and other evidences of hurry. One finds lumpy quotations, especially in the latter portion of the work, which a more leisurely writer would have digested. The friendly reviewer, however, can well overlook or condone such trifles, or even attribute a virtue to them. Thus George, Marquis of Halifax, said in a similar case: "He let his mind have its full flight, and showeth, by a generous kind of negligence, that he did not write for praise, but to give the world a true picture. . . . He scorned affected periods, or to please the mistaken reader with an empty chime of words. He . . . dependeth wholly upon the natural force of what is his own, and the excellent application of what he borroweth."

But even with these qualifications, the book is better literature than the average history; and it is certainly better history than the average journalist or even literary man produces. So far as notes, bibliographies, maps, charts, citations, etc., go, it is done well in the tradition of the scientific school. The work falls substantially within that definition which says that history is the recording and explaining of past events as steps in human progress, and authenticated study of the character and significance of events.

The Great Plains: A Study in Institutions and Environment, by Walter Prescott Webb, Associate Professor of History, The University of Texas. Ginn & Company, Boston. 1931. 525 pages. Price $4.00 (Texas orders should be addressed to Ginn & Co., Dallas.)